D1598361

One Stupid Mistake

Smart Decision-making in a Crazy World

By Charlie Seraphin

First Edition 2018

All rights reserved. No part of this book may be reproduced or transmitted in any form or by any electronic or mechanical means, including photocopying, recording or by any information storage and retrieval system, without the written permission of the Author, except where permitted by law.

© Charlie Seraphin, 2018

Website: OneStupidMistake.com

TABLE OF CONTENTS

Preface

You are standing on a ladder. Each time you make a decision you either go up or down. Good decisions lift you up a rung. Bad decisions push you down. This image represents our upward journey toward a goal. Not all decisions are equal. Great decisions raise you closer to your goal. Awful decisions can knock you off the ladder. Whether your goal is wealth, power, popularity, happiness, enlightenment or eternal salvation, your result is dependent on making good decisions.

Introduction

Nobody wants to make stupid mistakes, yet we all make them. This is a book about how and why we make mistakes, and what we can do to stop making them. Mistakes happen when we don't listen to ourselves. Whether it's the noise of the world, someone pushing us in the wrong direction, or just a lapse of consciousness, we forget to do the right thing. When we're distracted or not paying attention, we crash into the people and things around us. Bad decisions pile up like cars on a foggy highway. When we are aware of our thoughts, we are less likely to say or do stupid things.

You know the old saying "you are what you eat"? I've found that it's just as helpful to remember that "you are what you think." If your thinking is disjointed, chances are good you are making more than your share of stupid mistakes. Unfortunately, in order to embrace and learn from our mistakes, we need to understand how and why we make decisions, both good and bad. Just hoping to do better isn't enough. This little book will help you make smarter decisions and avoid stupid mistakes—especially the one stupid mistake that can ruin a life.

There are as many kinds of mistakes as there are personalities. Eduardo Briceño[1], the co-founder and CEO of Mindset Works, writes about several specific kinds of mistakes on his blog: stretch mistakes, aha-moment mistakes, sloppy mistakes, and high-stakes mistakes. There are also honest mistakes, careless mistakes, uncalculated mistakes, lazy mistakes, ignorant mistakes, beginner mistakes, systemic mistakes, and so on. Understanding all the various types of mistakes we make, however we classify them, helps us learn to avoid mistakes in the future. Whatever we call them, if they move us away from our goals, they impede our efforts to be happy.

Everybody makes mistakes. Mistakes are as natural as breathing. You probably don't consciously think about it when you breathe, and you definitely don't think about mistakes when you're making them. With practice, however, you can control both your breath and your decision making. In meditation we learn to concentrate on our inward breath. Breathe in slowly through your nose, filling your lungs with air. Exhale through your mouth, allowing stress to escape on your outward breath. Focused breathing relieves stress. Similarly, focused thinking eliminates mistakes. Just as we can become conscious of our breath as we breathe in and out, we can learn to control our thought process before we make stupid mistakes.

Have you ever thought about how many breaths you have left? Obviously we can't be sure which will be our last breath until we take it, but imagining that last breath can help us better understand good decision making. Mistakes are like breaths. Some people only stop and think about their stupid mistakes when they make the last one. What if your last breath is connected to your last stupid mistake? People die every day as a result of bad decisions. We hear their stories and wonder, "How could they have been so stupid?" But I'll bet you have done something and thought, "That was really stupid. I'm lucky I didn't get killed."

Making fewer mistakes and eliminating repeat mistakes requires a little thought, a little concentration, and a willingness to change. Regardless of how many times you've disappointed yourself, there's still hope. There aren't many pages here, and very few technical terms or complex ideas. You can read this whole book in less than two hours. When you've finished, you might want to go back and read each chapter as a meditation. There are twenty-one sections, so if you read one a day, you'll have exactly three weeks to work on eliminating stupid mistakes.

Depending on your own experiences, the stories may or may not jog memories, make you laugh, or make you cry. Some of the stories are more about somebody else than they are about you. If you've made a lot of bad decisions, like me, you'll relate to more of the stories.

Stories and memories give rise to emotions. Unfortunately emotions don't change behavior. Decisions, however, even small seemingly insignificant decisions, change lives. Do you fear making decisions? Do you make decisions without thinking? Do you overthink every decision? Regardless of what kind of person you are, good decisions are easy once you know how.

I've spent a lifetime studying (and making) stupid mistakes. I'm not a doctor or a psychologist, and I don't claim to be an expert who always makes the right decision. But I am a keen observer. I pay attention, and I've seen and experienced quite a few life crashes. I've also had many coaches, and I've done a lot of coaching. Good coaches help us make the most of our abilities. But in case you haven't noticed, life coaches don't always have the best life, strength coaches aren't always the strongest, and tennis coaches aren't the best tennis players. Knowing how to do something doesn't guarantee that you can do it well. In order to be good at anything, you need to know what to do and you need to be able to translate your knowledge into performance.

In order to understand, we must listen with a goal to understand. *Making good decisions requires listening.* Scientists use radio telescopes pointed at the sky to try to understand the creation of the universe. By listening, we can learn to understand ourselves. Our thoughts, words and our actions hold the keys to understanding. In order to move "up the ladder", you need simply to listen and learn. Listen to yourself, your thoughts, your words and everything you do in a critically constructive manner.

I like stories. We all enjoy a good story. Stories teach lessons. This book has lots of short stories about decisions. Good stories, good decisions and stupid mistakes all come from the same place. They start out as thoughts. My hope is that you'll connect some of the stories (and the lessons they teach) to your decisions. It's up to you to decide which stories are true, and which are fables.

What follows is a twenty-one day program focused on decisions. I built it with love. I've poured over each lesson a hundred times. It's simple and basic and intended to help you make your life better. If you make one more good decision each day, you can change your life. Take a deep breath, let it out slowly, and begin.

1. http://blog.mindsetworks.com/entry/mistakes-are-not-all-created-equal

CHAPTER ONE

What Was I Thinking?

Where do bad decisions come from? Why do we continually make stupid mistakes? Let's start by looking at my first stupid mistake.

Here's the first one I remember: I was six, standing on a crossbar near the top of a glider swing while two friends played below. The top of the glider had two metal tubes. When it went one direction, the hole in one tube opened, and when it went the other direction that hole pinched closed and the other side opened. Just before I put my finger into one of the holes a little voice said, "Don't do it. It's a bad idea." I tried to pull my finger out, but it was too late. Crushed between the metal tube and the metal frame, I got a nasty slice. A surgeon had to sew my finger back together. I still have a small scar and my right index finger goes numb when it's cold. Dumb decisions often have lasting consequences.

In simple terms, a stupid mistake is something we do even though we know better. Scientifically it's called cognitive dissonance—knowing better, but choosing to do the wrong thing anyway. When you and I (and famous people) do things we shouldn't, we're engaged in cognitive dissonance. When we lose touch with or ignore our inner voice, bad things happen. While I'll never again put my finger in a moving piece of equipment, I don't always learn from my mistakes. Serious pain helps us remember. If we do something stupid that makes us bleed, we are likely to remember not to do it again. Unfortunately, most bad decisions aren't accompanied by physical pain, so more often than not we repeat stupid mistakes.

Some mistakes take days, months and even years to manifest themselves. When we don't experience instant recognition of our error, things get even messier. As time passes, we may even deny that it was a bad decision.

Have you heard the philosophical question, "If a tree falls in the forest with no one to hear it, does it make a sound?" Some say yes, some say no. There are good arguments for both answers. Here's one you haven't heard, "Is it a stupid mistake if nobody knows (or finds out) what you did?" We can argue both sides of that question too. Some say, "No harm, no foul." Others suggest that we hold ourselves to a higher standard. Even if you're the only one who knows about your bad decision, it's always with you. You can bury it in your subconscious, but you can never erase it from your brain. Denying stupid mistakes can cause significant harm and have major, long term negative implications in your life.

Regardless of how you answer the question, you have to agree that our culture is disjointed by bad decisions. People behaving badly and doing stupid things is the new norm. High profile people lie, cheat, steal, molest, and make fools of themselves daily. Strangers indiscriminately murder innocents for no apparent reason. When combined with our own bad decisions, the world appears crazy. Sometimes we just want to hide and hope that it will all go away.

Don't give up hope. Take heart. Today is the first day of your personal program to diminish bad decisions and stupid mistakes. You and I are going to return sanity to our crazy world. We will balance chaos with honesty, integrity and personal responsibility. We are going to play a positive role in making the world a better place. We're going to eliminate stupid mistakes one at a time. If you stick with this simple program, you can eliminate one stupid mistake every day.

You may never have analyzed a stupid mistake before, but chances are good you remember decisions that you wish you hadn't made. When I asked people to recall one stupid mistake for this book, their first response was usually something like, "That's tough. There were so many!" But, believe it or not, every single person I've asked admitted that they have a little voice that tells them when they are about to do the wrong thing. Understanding our stupid mistakes, how and why we make them, helps us understand ourselves.

In my story, a little voice inside my head told me not to do it, but I did it anyway. As soon as I felt the pain and saw the blood, I knew it was a bad decision. How many times have you heard your little voice or had a nagging feeling that you shouldn't do something? As you read these accounts of decisions made by real people, you'll remember decisions that you've made, some recent, and others in your past. I'm asking you to spend time really thinking about your stupid mistakes. Although you'd never list mistakes and bad decisions on your resume, they are just as important as your accomplishments in determining who you are. Mistakes are like fingerprints. No two people are the same. We all do things that aren't in harmony with who we want to be. Some bad choices are visible—like the scar on my finger—but most stupid mistakes cannot be seen. Whether or not you list them on your resume, they continue to shape who you are.

Reflecting on and learning to understand stupid mistakes will help you stop being a victim of your past and allow you to become the person you want to be. As you journey through past decisions, you'll see and recognize behavior patterns. Pattern recognition and self-analysis are critical to eliminating stupid mistakes.

I don't want you to reflect on your mistakes to feel depressed or sad. My goal is to help you become aware of how you operate and how you behave in certain situations. We are all different, and we behave differently, but every one of us is the product of what we think, say, and do. We have some good and some bad.

If you want to learn to make more good decisions, you need to think more good thoughts. Down the road that may require altering your media consumption, the people you associate with and some other environmental elements, but for now we're simply going to begin remembering.

When you draft a resume, you order your accomplishments. As we begin this lesson, I'm going to ask you to order your mistakes. Remember as many as you can. Dig them up and examine them under a microscope. Juxtapose your stupid mistakes against who you want to be. In my seminars on personal brand development, I ask participants to list three words or phrases that describe their personal brand. Some are physical attributes (tall, short, dark, fair, handsome, beautiful) and others reflect character traits (optimistic, honest, trustworthy, funny, hardworking, etc.). At the end of the exercise, participants ask friends and relatives to write down words or phrases that characterize the participant's brand. It's no great surprise that few people get more than one supporting answer. Most people get no common descriptions, and nobody ever gets all three. The exercise demonstrates that we see ourselves differently than other people see us. We want them to see certain qualities, but often even our closest friends and loved ones see us very differently than we want them to see us.

Why is that? To begin with, others only hear our words and see our actions. They don't have access to our internal dialog. They don't hear us justifying what we do. They don't hear us comparing our actions to those of other people that we know, have read about or have seen on TV. What seems perfectly reasonable to us, doesn't always come off that way to others. If you're serious about improving and promoting your personal brand, and making fewer bad decisions, you need to think healthy, balanced thoughts. When you focus on your goals, positive words and actions flow naturally. You will be amazed at how quickly you can transform your life and project the personal brand attributes that you aspire to. You'll learn to make good decisions and avoid stupid mistakes.

You might be thinking, *But how do I control the things I think about? My mind just races from one thought to the next!* We all have bad habits. We are all subject to distractions. There is a lot of noise in our world. It's amazing there aren't even more stupid mistakes, considering all the chaos that surrounds us. But we don't have to be victims. We can take control of how we think, what we say, and how we act.

Good decision making requires a conscious effort. Understand that your thoughts are the forerunners of what you say and do. Recognizing the connection between thoughts and actions is basic. It's time to control your mind. Take charge of your thoughts. Focus on one thing at a time. If you haven't learned how to focus on one thing, try the exercise at the end of this chapter.

As you examine your decisions and the thoughts connected to them, you will begin to recognize the habits that are moving you toward your fate. Want fewer stupid mistakes? Dump your stupid thoughts, especially the recurring ones that distract you. Want to make better decisions? Listen to your little voice.

When I talk about your little voice, I'm not referring to the willy-nilly one that bounces around making noise in your head like a TV commercial. Your true internal voice is soft and quiet. It's like a gentle whisper. You may have to listen closely to hear it. You won't be able to hear it until you turn down the outside noise and learn to focus. In the meantime, it's up to you to sort through and separate good thoughts from bad thoughts. Your quiet little voice is your conscience. Awareness of your conscience is your ticket to a better life. Practice blocking out every other sound while you listen to your conscience. Once you forge the connection between your little voice and your choice of thoughts, cognitive dissonance and bad decisions will fade away. Very soon, when you hear that little voice warning you, "Don't do it!" you'll make the right decision.

If you like, you can make a notebook of thoughts associated with your mistakes. For example: I thought nobody would notice if I put it in my pocket and walked away. Or, I lied about my accomplishments because I wanted them to like me. Remember the mistake, and connect it to what you were thinking. Eventually you'll see a pattern between certain thoughts and stupid mistakes.

Wandering minds are the number one cause of accidents. Thinking about something in the past or the future causes us to neglect the present. Instead of being aware of what's happening in real time, our minds wander who knows where. Lack of focus results in bad decisions and stupid mistakes. If I asked you right after you cut your finger or bumped your head why you did it you'd probably respond, "I just wasn't thinking." The truth is that you were thinking about something other than what you were doing. Start remembering exactly what you were thinking when you messed up.

Have you noticed that when you are only focused on your own feelings, you tend to say things that hurt others' feelings? When we drown our sorrows in a bottle or take drugs "to settle our nerves," we say and do stupid things. Find the patterns associated with your mistakes. Connect your bad decisions to specific thoughts, feelings, people, situations, and actions. Reconstruct what you were thinking just prior to screwing up.

Learning to analyze your mistakes will help you shed them. Did you learn anything from your most serious stupid mistake? This is a step by step process. Let it resonate in your heart and in your mind. Unfortunately it's not a quick fix. Most of us have been making stupid mistakes for years. Unlearning bad habits will take some effort over a period of time, but you can do it. Commit some quiet time everyday to reflect on recent bad decisions. Turn them inside out. Don't beat yourself up, just work to understand what caused you to do what you shouldn't have done.

Listening meditation is an ancient exercise, and all that's required are ears and a desire to learn thought control. Later on we'll roll this exercise into practical everyday situations. Soon you'll be able to instantly control your thoughts and focus on your decisions. You'll make faster, better decisions without all the mental chatter that often distracts you. Remember, eliminating stupid mistakes begins with controlling the things we think about, and how we think about them. Take five minutes right now to begin your listening exercise. Close your eyes and just listen.

Exercise 1

Sit in a quiet space (it's better outdoors, but anywhere will do) and tell yourself that you're only going to think about listening for five minutes. Close your eyes and listen. Don't pay any attention to anything except what you hear. Try to identify all the sounds that are close, then push your mind to concentrate on sounds that are farther away. Listen for a sound that is the farthest away from where you are. Listen intently. Focus only on listening. If it's noisy, listen for the quiet sounds within the noise. If it's quiet, listen for the faintest sound. Start with five minutes today, just listening and forcing your mind to focus only on what you hear and no other thoughts. As you progress, lengthen the time you spend in quiet meditation. Train yourself to hear distant sounds. Remember, concentrate on the sounds. Let those sounds be your only thoughts.

Thought for the Day:
Just because I've made a thousand stupid mistakes doesn't mean I have to make one today.

CHAPTER TWO

Why Did I Do That?

As I look back now on my youthful mistakes, I knew better than to stick my finger in the metal pipe, swing by my legs from a tree branch, or try to push a hundred pound box up a ladder. I once told my little brother to stick his tongue on a frozen metal pole on a cold winter day. Why did I do that? He compounded my stupid mistake by listening to my suggestion. I felt terrible when he left a chunk of his tongue on the pole. Fifty years later, we still share that stupid mistake.

Immediately after recognizing a stupid mistake we usually ask, "Why did I do that?" Reflecting on my own stupid mistakes, the stupid mistakes that people have shared with me, and the ones I read about in each day's news, I've come to believe that we must have a stupid gene. A stupid gene is what pushes us to do dumb things, sometimes without thinking, and sometimes even after we've spent time deliberating our decision. Scientists may never isolate a stupid gene, but observation proves that it's somewhere in our DNA. For purposes of discussion, let's pretend that a genetic defect causes us to do certain stupid things.

One day you're having a conversation and a thought pops into your head and before you know it, it's out of your mouth. Then you look at the person you're talking with and their face tells you that it wasn't something that should have been said. Open mouth, insert foot. We've all done it, but some of us are more prone to stray remarks than others.

I remember being in a political science lecture in college and being overcome by the impulse to make a point. I impatiently raised my hand, interrupting the professor. "Yes, Mr. Seraphin, what is it?" he asked, somewhat exasperated by my interruption. I jumped to my feet and at that moment, my mind went blank. Whatever it was that I thought was so important had completely escaped me. I stood there in the middle of the lecture and started turning every shade of red. What had been so compelling one minute earlier was completely gone in a flash. All that remained was the embarrassment of having interrupted my professor's lecture.

When you break them down, stupid mistakes are often a function of acting before thinking. Instead of considering your audience and the impact of your words, or where you are and the potential impact of your action, you just let 'er fly. Before you know it you've hurt somebody's feelings or embarrassed yourself with an inappropriate comment (or brain freeze) or done something that causes pain. The fix is obvious, but it takes some willpower along with a desire to eliminate foot-in-mouth disease. Get a grip and you can overcome your stupid gene and keep from falling into the quicksand.

The same goes for written communication, especially a hasty text, tweet, or email. Sometimes our desire to communicate a thought overrides our deliberative process. We hit the send key before we proofread the message.

If your life is full of regretful comments and written correspondence (like mine) it could be that we need to slow down. If you are accident prone or if you consistently choose the wrong course of action, slow down. Rushing through life is fraught with danger! Traffic accidents and physical injuries aside, speed causes serious problems with communication. Here are three simple rules to follow:

1) *If you're talking to someone in person, look at them while they are speaking.* I mean really look

at them. Listen carefully to what they are saying (be an active listener) and then keep looking at them as you respond. Your eye contact will help guide you away from careless words that cause pain. Using your eyes and ears to augment your brain will help you from falling into the stupid trap. In the lecture example, I should have written my "important thought" in my notes. If I had continued listening to the lecture, the professor might have answered my question. If not, I could have discussed it with him at an appropriate time after class. Talking to (or shouting at) someone in another room is another technique guaranteed to lead to miscommunication. If you can't see the person you're talking to, there's a good chance they can't clearly hear what you're saying.

2) *If you're talking with someone by phone, find a place to sit or stand where you can concentrate on what's being said.* You're much less likely to blurt out a thoughtless, hurtful or stupid comment if you're really involved in listening and communicating. Distractions cause accidents. When you're behind the wheel there is as much danger on the other end of a conversation as there is in front of or behind your vehicle. Driving is not a good time to have a serious telephone conversation. Talking on the phone or texting when you're in the checkout line at a store or when you're in a restaurant can also be a prelude to a thoughtless, stupid comment (not to mention it's rude to employees, other customers, and fellow shoppers and diners).

3) *If you're texting or writing an email, read what you've written before hitting the send button.* It's best to read it aloud so your ears can filter the real meaning of the words you're writing, but even if you're in a place that doesn't allow you to read aloud, read it carefully before you send it. If it's an especially important email or one that might cause problems down the road, it's better to save it as a draft and return to it in an hour or two—or even better, the next day. When you read it aloud after a period of rest and reflection, you are likely to strengthen the meaning, and perhaps soften the tone as you choose your words more carefully. I have a bad habit of writing snarky emails. In the moment, it always feels like the right thing to do. Get it off my chest, I tell myself. Set the record straight, and put them in their place. But most times sending an email with lots of attitude is a bad idea. I've created family feuds, hurt countless people's feelings and even cost myself a job. If you feel strongly about writing a harsh email, at least give yourself twenty-four hours to reconsider before you hit the send button.

Whether it's a word coming out of your mouth, or a thoughtless action, failing to use your brain leads directly to stupid mistakes. Once you get in touch with your little voice, the one that may have been drowned out by the noise of your adult world, you can begin to envision not only your thoughts, words, and actions but the impact that they're likely to have on your life and the lives of others.

We are imperfect people. Emails, texts and tweets are imperfect forms of communication. Writing instead of talking is a recipe for misunderstanding. You may know what you're feeling and what you mean to say, but the written word is often misinterpreted. *"When in doubt, leave it out!"*

Schedule a face to face meeting, or at least pick up the phone and have a conversation. And while we're on the subject, don't stick your nose where it's not welcomed. Even if you believe strongly that the points you are making are true and honest, more likely than not, the folks you're addressing aren't interested in your comments and criticisms. Here's a simple litmus test: Is what you're saying or doing likely to make others feel better? Is what you're communicating likely to change their mind or change their course of action? Is what you're communicating moving you or the other person up the ladder of enlightenment? Or are you just venting? Most of the time, it's the latter.

Exercise 2

Remember the last time a text, email or words from your mouth got you into trouble? Recreate the situation and think about better ways you might have communicated your thoughts and feelings. Try to remember what you were thinking and feeling just before you hit the send button or blurted out the words that caused the problem. Do you still have those thoughts and feelings? Did what you said result in any benefit to you or anyone else? Is there another way of looking at the issue? Can you think of better words to express those same thoughts and feelings? Turn it around and imagine how you would feel if you were the one receiving the communication. Honest analysis of our mistakes helps us develop a plan of action. So slow down, think it through (from all perspectives), and imagine a similar situation in the future. Close your eyes and think about a disagreement or potential confrontation. How can you better communicate your thoughts and feelings in a balanced, controlled manner? What can you say that will get the message through without burning down the house? *Preparation is the key to communication.* Taking time to rethink your message, your choice of words and your message delivery system are critical first steps toward avoiding errant communication.

Practice your listening exercise again. Spend time on each sound, starting with the sound closest to you and working your way toward the most distant sound. Notice that new sounds will appear, but keep listening for the furthest sound. Keep your eyes closed and your ears open for five minutes.

Thought for the Day:
When in doubt, leave it out. Hold that thought!

CHAPTER THREE

If I Had It To Do Over Again

Mike is a dentist who was married to a woman named Janice. He and Janice didn't get along. They argued and bickered until they decided to divorce. Mike dated for a while, and then announced that he had found the perfect woman. He was in love. Ironically, the new love of his life was also named Janice. As fate would have it, she shared a birthday and many personality traits with Mike's first wife. Can you see where this is going? A short while later, Mike announced that he was extracting himself from another failed marriage.

The saying goes, "You never get a second chance to make a first impression." In like manner, it's always better to get it right the first time. Blowing it and having to make a recovery isn't fun. Pulling life out of the ashes is doable (see Chapter 15), but it's a whole lot easier if you pay attention the first time.

Why do we keep making the same stupid mistakes? Besides blaming the hard to isolate stupid gene, ego and arrogance play a major role for repeat offenders. Repeating an action and expecting a different outcome is by definition insanity, yet many perfectly sane people do exactly that. Unfortunately they don't ask themselves, "Why am I doing this again?" They wait till the disappointing outcome and ask, "Why did I do that... again?" How many of us continue to repeat the same stupid mistakes? If we weren't convinced that we can force a different outcome from the same actions, we wouldn't try, but some mysterious force seems to push us to defy logic. When we're in the middle of a stupid repeat mistake, we don't even recognize how illogically we're behaving even though in the scheme of life, *repeated mistakes never produce happy outcomes.*

Here's a good rule: If it didn't work before, (and nothing has changed) it's not likely to work now.

Ross has always wanted desperately to have a romantic relationship. He gets shy around women and freezes up when he finds himself attracted to someone. Whenever Ross gets into a situation where he could begin to develop a relationship, he either clams up, does something totally dorky, or says something inappropriate. When we've talked about it, his excuse is that other people are good with the opposite sex, but he's not. He's a wonderful person, and he has accomplished much in life, but he appears headed to his grave as single and unattached. There's nothing wrong with being alone, but based on what he has told me, that's not what is in Ross's heart of hearts. So why does Ross repeatedly sabotage his desire to become involved in a relationship, and how can he remedy the problem?

Avoiding stupid mistakes in relationships is often a function of paying attention and learning from our previous mistakes. If you've been in a failed relationship (or relationships) step back and take a look at who, what and why. Can you remember what you were thinking and feeling when you first entered into the relationship? Did you have realistic expectations? Were your eyes wide open? I've heard people say that their partner changed dramatically after they became engaged or married, but in my experience people don't change as much as our observations and expectations change.

When we first meet someone, we tend to look past the very flaws that later drive us crazy. We get so caught up in the moment that we don't really consider compatibility issues. We become romantically starstruck and fail to see faults that we aren't prepared to accept in a partner. We project the image of what we want in a partner onto another person rather than paying attention to who that other person really is. Being committed to a long-term relationship requires a conscious decision to accept others' flaws. Hopefully you have a clear and unfettered idea of who it is that you're committing to, but odds are good that there are habits, characteristics and personality flaws that you've overlooked in your zeal to become romantically involved. Thinking that you've found a perfect mate is a stupid mistake. There are no perfect humans. We've all got baggage, and we're all flawed. It's the conscious decision to accept others flaws as we continue to address our own that provides the best chance for relationship success.

Ross can't find a perfect partner because he can't get past self-criticism and accept himself as the imperfect guy that he is. He normally thinks that the objects of his affection are much too good for him, so he bows out before even beginning the dance. Other people I know "dance" with everyone they meet and can't understand why serious relationships just don't seem to work out for them. Sometimes being smart and clever is just as ineffective as being shy. There's a time and a place for everything, and the time and place for relationship development are not always determined by you.

The key to avoiding stupid relationship mistakes is similar to avoiding any other sort of stupid mistake. It starts with awareness. Awareness of ourselves, our qualities and imperfections comes first. Awareness of the qualities and imperfections of others comes next. Awareness of our past, our history, especially our relationship history is important. Don't dwell on the stupid relationship mistakes you've made before, but be aware of what you thought, said and did that might have contributed to their failure. Be aware of everyone in your life. What you think about them is as important as what you feel about them. There's a difference. Thoughts and feelings are especially important in relationships. I'm not suggesting that you should over-analyze every potential relationship, but if you're serious about someone, be serious. Physical attraction is a strong force. It can't, however, assure a meaningful, lasting relationship. Intellectual compatibility is important, but it doesn't guarantee a successful relationship. Emotional compatibility is a better measure of potential relationship success than either physical or intellectual attraction.

People who put time and effort into choosing their thoughts, words and actions tend to make fewer relationship mistakes. There are computer dating services that can perform the analysis for you, but ultimate relationship happiness is up to you. Know yourself, get to know the other person, and pay attention as you go through the friendship/mating ritual. In a recent study, dating websites report that although some clients list attributes of the perfect mate, most are more than happy to meet people who bear no resemblance to their "ideal" partner. Your mother may have told you that you'll know when you've found the right one. She was right, but she might not have explained how much work goes into holding a relationship together once you realize that your partner isn't perfect. Remember: We're all flawed. Nobody is perfect. We all make stupid mistakes.

Being empathetic, interested in and concerned about the thoughts and feelings of others is a wonderful antidote for stupid interpersonal mistakes. Pay attention. Stop thinking exclusively about yourself and pay attention to those whom you are trying to impress.

Exercise 3

Practice your listening exercise. Listen for the far away sound and then work your way back to the sound closest to your ears. Listen for the loudest sound, and then listen for the most quiet sound that you can barely hear. Close your eyes. Be still.

Thought for the Day:
Before you begin to remove the splinter from another's eye, consider the log that is blocking your own vision.

CHAPTER FOUR

Quick Fixes and Bad Results

Bob and Ellen live in the Hollywood Hills with their three cats. Ellen repeatedly reminded Bob to be sure the door was closed so their cats wouldn't get outside, especially the timid one. One day Bob forgot. "I don't know what I was thinking," he explained. It was a stupid mistake. The cat escaped and was eaten by a coyote. Bob felt awful. Not only did his mistake cost him a cat, it really upset Ellen, so Bob rushed out to get another cat to replace the one they lost. Bob calls the replacement, "the cat from hell." It shreds furniture, rugs and clothing, refuses to use the litter box, and generally makes life miserable.

Sometimes we compound our mistakes with bad "corrective" decisions that lead to more problems. Sometimes we blame others for our bad decisions. Sometimes we pretend that we're not connected to bad decisions that we've made. In order to learn from a stupid mistake, we have to acknowledge it. Trading it for something else or sweeping it under the rug won't make it go away.

Terry is a retired football player. One day he was sitting in his living room smoking a cigar and telling a small group of us a story. It was a long story, and the ash on Terry's cigar got longer and longer. Before the story ended, the ash fell on the white shag carpet. Terry was animated. We were spellbound. Rather than interrupt his story to pick up the ash, Terry reached out with his bare left foot and smushed the ash into the carpet. It was a very funny story, but the memory of watching Terry rub black cigar ash into white shag carpet is funnier than the story. He was so intent on finishing his story that he fixed his mistake by making it worse.

Stupid mistakes are avoidable. So why do we make so many bad decisions? What makes us forget to close the door or use the ashtray? Do we just get so carried away with ourselves and what we're thinking about that we forget to pay attention to what we know is right? How can we begin to eliminate most if not all of our stupid mistakes? How can we keep from compounding our mistakes?

First, let's imagine what would happen if you eliminated stupid mistakes and did only the right things, or at least, the things you thought were right. Try to envision a time when you will always be thoughtful, when you will stay in the moment and concentrate on what you are thinking, saying, and doing. Be determined that from now on, you will make good decisions. Now, take a minute, step back, and reflect on your most recent stupid mistake. What were the circumstances? What did you do? What should you have done? What were the consequences? How do you intend to avoid that same stupid mistake going forward? Is your plan realistic? Can you remember an instance when you compounded a simple mistake and made it even worse?

Remember that smart people make mistakes just as frequently as dumb people. Smart people try to cover their tracks, but many brilliant people have made and continue to make really dumb decisions. Movie moguls, politicians, athletes, and TV personalities have all recently been decimated by the arrogance of their repeated stupid actions. It would have been so easy for them to avoid their tragic falls from grace. The first time they did what they knew was wrong, they could have apologized, taken the heat and asked for forgiveness. In our culture, first-time offenders are normally given the benefit of the doubt. Even if they would have been chastised, their punishment wouldn't be nearly as severe as it is today. Instead of being honest with themselves, they put their selfish, lustful wants above good judgement. Each of them drowned out the "little voice" of their conscience with the cacophony of their ego. They never expected to get caught, and they envisioned themselves too smart, too powerful, and too popular to fall. Now, we all know their names, and they will be forever associated with their stupid mistakes.

Making consistently good decisions starts with little decisions. Pay attention to everything. Create good decision habits by thinking positive thoughts and then following through by doing the things you're supposed to do. When that stupid thought pops into your head, dismiss it with a thought that is more consistent with your character. Be who you want to be, not the jerk who poses for stupid pictures or takes advantage of others. But you won't be able to avoid the big bad decisions if you don't start with self-discipline in little, simple decisions.

There are lots of little things that you can do every day to develop good habits. Take the time to make your bed, close the door behind you, put things back where you got them and clean up after yourself. Self-discipline is a great place to practice thought control. I'm thinking it, and I'm doing it, and it's exactly what I know I should be doing.

Exercise 4

Practice your listening exercise and try to
listen for seven minutes. Remember to focus
only on what you hear. Train your mind
to think only "hearing thoughts." You're
becoming more mindful, and less forgetful.
Congratulate yourself on your progress.

Thought for the Day:
*Doing the right things, the right way, for the right
reasons, puts you in the best position to avoid stupid
mistakes and live a healthy, happy life.*

CHAPTER FIVE

Raise Your Hand If It's Your Fault

Dick was a bright young man with a bright future. While he wasn't the smartest, the richest, or the most talented, his tenacious nature helped him overcome many obstacles. He faced each defeat with a new determination and eventually became a U.S. senator. His fast-track political career put him in position to be chosen as a candidate for vice president. He was elected and served two terms. After suffering a bitter defeat in his first run for president, he came back eight years later and won the presidency. Dick became the most powerful man in the world—until his stupid mistakes undid him.

Despite his many accomplishments, Dick is most famous for trying to cover up a stupid mistake. Instead of admitting that his subordinates had done something stupid (and illegal), he tried to make it go away. He erased tapes of his office conversations. He did everything in his power to conceal the truth. His ill-advised decision to try to cover his tracks eventually cost him his presidency and cemented his place in history as "Tricky Dick."

Richard Nixon's attempt to cover up the Watergate scandal is a tragedy of historic proportion. Nixon wasn't forced to resign because his supporters and senior staff ordered a break-in, but because Nixon lied in an effort to conceal their involvement. By itself, the Watergate break-in would have been a footnote in American history. But his effort to cover up a stupid mistake resulted in the resignation of a president.

Bill had a bad complexion as a young man. He came from the wrong side of the tracks and was never as popular, especially with girls, as he wanted to be. After law school he became a successful politician and enjoyed a new popularity. He too rose to the highest position of power in the free world. He used his position and power to take advantage of women. Then he lied about having sex with an intern at the White House. Like Nixon, Bill Clinton was accused of obstruction of justice. Although he wasn't forced to resign, his legacy is also forever stained.

Stupid mistakes don't happen in a vacuum, and sooner or later, the world will know. The more we work to hide our mistakes, the more likely it is that the cover-up will add to the severity of the consequences. Stupid mistakes become like cancerous tumors. They fester and grow. Each step of the coverup digs a deeper hole. Whether it's White House tapes revealed, or "a blue dress" coming out of the closet, sooner or later the truth will surface. Cover-ups become transparent in light. As lies are exposed, humiliation fills the void. Please remember that if it can happen to the most powerful people in the world, it can happen to you. You can run, but you can't hide from the truth. Your bad decisions will hunt you down, and sooner or later, the truth will prevail.

Remembering how we got away with something in the past (without getting caught) compounds our problem. How many times have you had someone explain that it wasn't what you did that hurt them, it was that you lied about doing it? By trying to convince ourselves that our behavior will yield favorable results, by counting on our cunning and deceitfulness to cover our tracks, we begin the spiral that can only end in sadness and defeat. Justifications are excuses. Excuses are only necessary when we make the wrong decision. Cognitive dissonance, doing what we instinctively know is wrong, always becomes a stupid mistake.

If you find yourself thinking about how you will explain your decision to others, chances are good that you are already involved in cognitive dissonance. When you make good decisions, justification isn't necessary. When you make good decisions, you don't have to give them a second thought.

In today's media-dominated world, the problems associated with making stupid mistakes are magnified. We all make stupid mistakes. Unfortunately, because of digital technology and social media, today's mistakes have a longer shelf-life than mistakes of previous eras. YouTube, Facebook, Twitter and Instagram provide a daily chronicle of stupid mistakes. There are cameras and microphones everywhere. Nearly everything you say and do is being recorded, and has the potential to be publically broadcast.

You can see the effects of this new era everywhere. Another president, Donald Trump, said and did some stupid things, and his recorded history almost caused him to lose the election. His words and actions also cost him the respect of many Americans.

A famous golfer ruined his brand by cheating on his wife. He had projected the image of a family man, a good guy. Facts revealed that he was neither. He tried to cover his stupid mistakes with lies and eventually the bottom fell out of his world.

A powerful movie producer was finally exposed after years of predatory sexual behavior. Famous TV personalities, executives and politicians are daily being rooted out for their past indiscretions. They thought they were impervious to revelation. They thought they were above the law. They thought they would never be caught. They knew what they did was wrong, but they convinced themselves that their celebrity and power would protect them from the truth. As the old saying goes, the truth hurts.

On the other side of social media, women who pose for nude photos intended only for loved ones surface publicly every day. When they posed they overruled their better judgement. They convinced themselves that it would be OK, even though they had a feeling that something might go wrong. When lovers fall out of love, they often do mean things like having "revenge sex" or putting up salacious photos of their ex-lovers on the internet. Nobody can be trusted to cover your stupid mistakes.

Each of us has said and done things that we wish we hadn't. We've all been the victims of our own stupid mistakes. Many times our mistakes are private. Driving down a deserted highway, a piece of loose paper blows out an open window. It's gone, and we keep driving. Sometimes we roll up the window if there are more papers in the car. Sometimes we feel guilty for miles. We didn't intend to litter, but we littered. If a state trooper pulls you over for littering, it's best to admit what happened and apologize. It's when we try to cover our mistakes with lies that we get into deeper trouble. Trying to convince him that envelope with your name came from another vehicle is a bad decision.

You don't have to be president or a national celebrity to suffer the consequences of a failed cover-up. A quiet moment of reflection will help you recall a situation where you tried to cover a mistake. Nine times out of ten, even if your cover was successful, you carry some degree of guilt for having lied or intentionally led others away from the truth. This may be the easiest solution in the book.

The best time to fix a stupid mistake is before you make it! Making better decisions is a whole lot easier than covering your tracks and deflecting attention away from your actions. At the very least, when you do something dumb, when you make a stupid mistake, own it. The world is very forgiving of a person who owns up to his or her mistakes. Since we all make mistakes, we're likely to accept an honest apology following a misstep. But lying, deflecting, and hiding from the truth are universally unacceptable. Even if you cover your tracks, one day, sooner or later, time will expose the truth. The weight of a lie gets heavier with every breath. Truth is a powerful ally. It's so simple, but it may be the most important reflection in this book.

Exercise 5

Take a few minutes to examine your conscience.
Resolve to be honest and truthful, even when
you've made an embarrassing mistake. If you're
carrying guilt, find a way to make it right. As
difficult as it is, especially if you've been lying
for a considerable period of time, the day you
admit the truth is the day you'll be free.

Today is a good day to move your listening
exercise to a new location. Start by listening
close and then listen for the faintest sound you
can hear. Stay with that sound. Examine it. Give
it color and shape and make it as clear as you
can. Try to see (in your mind's eye) what you are
hearing. Your listening exercise is helping you
connect with your inner voice. Just taking seven
minutes away from everything except your
desire to hear things in your environment is a
huge accomplishment.

Thought for the Day:
*The pain of admission and apology are less than the
eternal weight of waiting to be exposed.*

CHAPTER SIX

The Company You Keep

Billy went to the store with a group of his friends. Jack had the bright idea that they would spread out and each one would put something in his pocket and walk out without paying. It was a dumb idea, and Billy didn't feel good about it, but he went along. Peer pressure can be powerful. Billy didn't realize that the owner of the store was on to them the minute they walked in. He watched Billy put a candy bar in his pocket and walk out. By the time Billy got home, his mother was waiting for him with a switch. She spanked him. Then she made Billy return to the store and apologize to the store owner. She made Billy work cutting lawns until he repaid the store ten times the value of the candy he stole. His mother knew that Jack was the ringleader and she assured Billy that the next time she saw that kid, she was going to let him have it. Billy learned a valuable lesson. He told Jack that he wasn't allowed to hang out with him anymore. The story has a thousand variations, but the lesson is always the same.

There are often people in our lives who bring out the worst in us. Whether they come from fractured homes or wonderful families, some people are just prone to leading us into bad situations. Every one of us has had a friend who was trouble. You know exactly what I'm talking about. It's the person who, regardless of the situation, pushes the envelope. It may be something as simple as smoking cigarettes or going to sleazy places. When we get together, we tend to do things that aren't consistent with the image we want to portray. When we're with that person, we smoke a cigarette, tell off-color jokes, or say things that we wouldn't repeat in front of people we respect. Whether it's bad language, drinking, doing drugs, or reckless behavior, we've all known someone that tends to lead us counterclockwise. It's not that these friends are bad people, per se, it's just that they tend to bring out our worst behavior.

It may not be easy, but it's time to start distancing yourself from them and their compromising behavior. It will take a lot of courage to tell them that you don't want to associate with them because you are charting a higher course for your life, but some of you are up to the task. If you can't muster the strength to tell them the truth, don't lie and make excuses. (We know how that usually works out.) Just make yourself unavailable to them; stop going to the places you're likely to see them and start creating distance. They'll figure out that you've made a decision to change your behavior, and if they want to be your friend, they'll have to clean up their act and come up to your standards.

Back when communities across America were tighter knit, neighbors kept an eye on one another. Parents raised children, but the village helped create social order. In my neighborhood, my parents called out neighbors' children as frequently as they disciplined me. It didn't matter if it was your parents or the parents of someone down the street. People weren't afraid to step up and let you know if they saw you doing something you shouldn't be doing. Because people knew one another, even in neighborhoods in larger cities, there weren't many strangers. When somebody did something wrong, the trail of evidence wasn't hard to follow. Justice was swift and harsh. If children got into trouble at school, they were in worse trouble when they got home. Parents knew teachers personally, and they formed a strong net that didn't allow anybody to fall through.

Today's mega-schools don't allow for that same personal

connection. Parents and teachers don't always know students, and it's relatively easy for troubled individuals and troublemakers to avoid detection. Unless they act out and draw attention to themselves in front of authorities, they go undetected. And there seem to be more troublemakers and troubled individuals, so there are more opportunities to find yourself with someone who is a bad influence.

At work, we sometimes encounter people who may pass the minimum requirements of the job, but their behavior doesn't make the grade. Whether it's slacking, wasting time, or destroying company property on the job, certain individuals always seem to be attached to trouble. Hanging with them, even if they are the "in crowd," is a recipe for stupid mistakes. Whether you are guilty or not, sooner or later you'll get drawn into their problem. Ray Barnett, who was the best boss I ever had, often said, "Never make another person's problem your problem!" That was good advice.

It's hard these days to make social decisions based on principle. It's not easy to walk away from the crowd, even when it's obvious that they are headed in the wrong direction. You may be a solid person who learned good values from your parents, or you may come from a dysfunctional home with no direction. Either way, there's no excuse for being anything less than the good person you were meant to be. If it doesn't come naturally, you may have to work at it, but since you were motivated enough to read a book about stupid mistakes, you have what it takes to choose the high road.

Unfortunately too many of today's parents make excuses for their children, award them with participation trophies, and fail to teach "old fashioned" values. They raise children by plopping them in front of a TV or computer. Early education is too often left to game designers and programmers. Parents abdicate their parental responsibilities. Instead of tolerance and respect, we see entitled individuals who believe the world revolves around them. Impatience and intolerance spread like wildfire.

The deterioration of family structure and values manifests itself in many forms of bad behavior. Many contemporary Americans choose heroes based solely on economic or athletic accomplishment. Other "heroes" are spoiled, self-centered, narcissists who are best known for their exceptionally stupid mistakes. Celebrity far exceeds morality, work-ethic, courage or decision-making ability. Misbehavior and social chaos are commonplace. Sensationalistic magazines and news programs offer never-ending coverage of celebrities doing stupid things. Instead of being punished for bad decisions, dozens of knuckle-heads become media stars. It's the new normal for famous people to behave badly, which encourages kids to do the same.

The problem is exacerbated by social media. Instead of kids getting in trouble and the story having a short shelf-life, today's stupid mistakes are forever enshrined in the Cloud—easily accessible and ripe for mass distribution. In today's world, the stupid mistake you made five years ago is only one digital click away. *With the internet full of our stupid mistakes, good decision-making is more important now than ever.*

The old saying is, "You're often judged by the company you keep." I'm not so concerned about you being judged as I am about you compromising your values because of peer pressure. Are you making bad decisions because you're hanging with people that you know you shouldn't be associating with? This isn't just aimed at young people. There are many middle aged adults and seniors who face the same dilemma. You lack the courage to separate from people that you know bring out the worst in your character.

Our ancestors were God-fearing people. Many of them did the right thing because of their fear of eternal damnation. Most people today don't have that fear. We aren't afraid of repercussions from peers, parents, or employers. Very few are afraid of losing eternal salvation. Some have no experience with parental punishment (or any other type of authoritarian discipline). Living in the moment with little or no thought about future consequences drives many of today's decisions.

The lack of family structure and moral values creates increasing challenges. The deterioration of moral standards and the growth of secular culture are exacerbating the growth of cognitive dissonance and drowning out the voice of reason. Decisions are driven by fads. Traditional heroes and positive role models are replaced by shallow, entertainment icons.

Making good personal decisions in a crazy world is the only antidote for stupid mistakes. Our stupid gene and the tools of good decision making are both embedded in our DNA. Sometimes it's hard to get to the core of your moral self. Sometimes the noise of the world drowns out the little voice that distinguishes good from evil and right from wrong. We've become numb to inhumane stupid mistakes. We long to celebrate authentic heroes with strong moral codes and values, because they are increasingly rare. That's why you and I need to elevate our behavior. It's time for you to become an authentic hero.

You have a choice. You can follow the crowd over the cliff without regard for good decision making, or you can stand up and take responsibility for your actions. *Each of us is in control of, and ultimately responsible for our fate.* We can blame our circumstance, environment or parents. We can blame our stupid mistakes on teachers, coaches, bosses and "friends." We can point the finger in a million different directions, but at the end of the day, each of us is responsible for what we think, what we say, what we do, and the image we project (through pictures and written words). Excuses are excuses. Your stupid mistakes can't be assigned to anybody—nobody but you.

Exercise 6

Your listening exercise today is about relaxation. Forget all your problems for a few minutes by sitting quietly with your eyes closed and listening. Beyond the mechanical sounds are comforting sounds. Lock in on a natural sound and stay with it. You're moving in the right direction. You can make a difference. Don't give up. You're a lot stronger than you think. Close your eyes and begin. There are many wonderful sounds waiting to be heard.

Thought for the Day:
You are what you think, say and do. Thanks to you, our world just became a better place.

CHAPTER SEVEN

What Happened to the Bees?

Tom raises bees in central Wisconsin. It's a hobby. He enjoys his hives. When the bees are productive, Tom has plenty of honey for himself, his friends and neighbors. But last summer Tom lost his hives. He doesn't remember doing anything differently than the year before, but the bees disappeared and the hives collapsed. Tom was concerned that he had done something wrong, but he checked and double-checked, and he was pretty sure that he hadn't made any stupid mistakes. The bees were just gone.

Honey bees pollinate eighty percent of the world's food supply. Across the globe countries are reporting significant and, in some cases, catastrophic declines in bee populations. The experts call it CCD: colony collapse disorder. Bees simply fail to return to their hives. They disappear, and their bodies are never found. Scientists have known for some time that pesticides and other man-made contaminants are decimating the global bee population, but recent scientific experiments have uncovered a new problem. CCD is now being linked to wireless communication.

Bees have a membrane behind their eyes that functions as an electromagnetic homing device. It allows them to wander off for miles in search of nectar and still find their way back to the hive. The rapid growth of wireless technology and construction of enormous cellular transmitting towers are disrupting the bees' natural ability to find their way home. When bees can't find their way home, they die. Scientists have tested the theory by putting wireless phones on or near beehives. When active wireless phones are present, bees refuse to enter their hives. In other words, cell phones bug bees.

Is it a coincidence that the technology that has captured the attention of our generation may be killing a critical link in the food chain? Could the miracle technology that allows us to communicate instantaneously around the globe be threatening the miracle of honey bees and pollination? Can we breed a new bee species that is immune to the negative effect of cell phone transmission frequencies? Can we be more sensitive to the placement of wireless transmission towers? And what does all this have to do with eliminating stupid mistakes?

Think about your daily routine. There are forces affecting you that you can't see and never consider. Cancer, Alzheimer's, autism and other diseases, stress, terrorism, murder and other violent crimes and abnormalities are increasing across the planet and nobody is offering an explanation, much less a solution. Some suggest that it's just modern living in a technological age, an outcome caused by population growth and evolution. Some suggest that it's a natural form of population control. Others believe what's happening is unnatural and that we're in the process of exterminating our species.

Good decisions minimize stupid mistakes. Individual accountability plays an enormous role not only in your wellbeing, but in the future well- being of the planet. I'm not saying that serious disease and planetary chaos is entirely caused by stupid mistakes, but it's worth remembering that environmental pollution, processed food, and unhealthy living conditions are regularly tied to cancer and other diseases. Stressing over stupid decisions can cause heart disease. Depression, addiction, violent behavior and many other maladies and abnormalities are directly related to bad choices. Healthy lifestyle decisions can't insure against disease, but eliminating stupid dietary mistakes and choosing to exercise is a start. We can't control everything in our environment, but controlling the things we can control through healthy choices dramatically increases our physical well-being and mental health.

The decline of honey bee populations demonstrates that there are forces at work in our environment that are affecting our quality of life. Forging ahead without regard for implications and outcomes is dangerous. If stupid mistakes continue to proliferate, future generations may never taste honey. GPS on our phones may help us find our way home, but too many of us aren't seeing, much less smelling, the flowers along the way.

What changed in the past two minutes since you checked your phone? What is the sum total of the value you received by becoming a slave to your personal device? Is your life fuller, better, richer since you became addicted to instant communication and social media? Are you and your friends closer, happier, healthier and wealthier because of your technology ties? Are we willing to exchange cell phone technology for intimate conversations? Do you find yourself sitting at dinner across from someone who is texting? Is your human interaction being filtered through a device? When is the last time you watched a honey bee or a hummingbird pollinating a flower? Have you ever experienced either of those things? Try to be more cognizant of the world around you, and you will have a happier, healthier life.

Exercise 7

Your exercise today is more difficult. Turn your phone off for one hour. Spend that time outdoors. Realize that more mistakes and accidents happen indoors than outdoors in the light of day. During your hour, devote at least ten minutes to quiet reflection. As you close your eyes and listen, separate the manmade mechanical sounds from natural sounds. Focus on natural sounds. Listen to the wind, the rustling of the trees, the sound of water or whatever nature provides in your immediate environment. Stretch your hearing to take in a distant bird, or if you are really fortunate, the sound of a honey bee.

Thought for the Day:
There's a reason peace and quiet go together.

CHAPTER EIGHT

A Crash Course in Spinning (Out of Control)

Tony was a thinker, a writer, and a doer. He wrote a number of books and lectured around the world. His students and fans loved him. Many of his contemporaries misunderstood him. He was often in trouble with his superiors, and after his death, his superiors cautioned that his teachings were not in line with established doctrine. He liked to push the envelope. He told his audiences to feel. He constantly asked heavy questions like, "How would you describe the color green to a blind man?" and "How would you describe the smell of a fragrant rose to someone who has never encountered a rose?" By asking people to feel, Tony made them think.

Unfortunately, many people don't like thinking. Tony was a lot like the guy in the old proverb. It describes a man standing outside at night pointing up into the sky. The proverb says, "When a wise man points to the moon, a fool sees only his finger." It's a shame Tony didn't get his message to a broader audience. He died of a heart attack at 55. My favorite quote from Anthony DeMello is, "Don't ask the world to change. You change first."

Is there room in your high-speed transmission world for silent reflection? Are you prepared to take twenty minutes a day for meditation or an examination of conscience? How many of your stupid mistakes are the result of moving too fast, multitasking, or simply not paying attention to what you are thinking, saying or doing?

Did you text while driving today? Were you looking at your phone while in the presence of someone you love? Have you learned that multitasking is a sure way to do more than one job poorly? Have you figured out yet that thinking one thing while doing another leads to disjointed thoughts and screwed up actions.

Life is full of boobie traps. My attic has a low ceiling, and nails from the roof stick down through the roof boards. When I walk in my attic, I have to stoop down to make sure I don't hit my head on one of those nails. I've been in my attic a hundred times. When I focus on where I am and what I'm doing there I have no problem with the overhead nails. When I daydream, or think about another project I'm working on, I invariably feel the sharp prick of a nail on my head. I've done it a dozen times, and every time I hit a nail (with my head) I remember that I wasn't paying attention.

Unfortunately not all of life's boobie traps are as sharp as the nails in my attic. When we daydream, lose focus and trip the traps there might not be instant pain to bring us back to the moment. In fact, sometimes we go for hours, days or weeks without even noticing that we're in the wrong place, doing the wrong thing. Sooner or later, when the proverbial shit hits the fan, we are forced to acknowledge that we were going through the motions without really paying attention. The damage is done. As much as I dislike those nails that hold the shingles on my roof, when I'm in the attic, I'm grateful that they help keep the rain out and keep me alert.

That might seem counterintuitive. You might think that because I hit my head on nails, I wouldn't like nails sticking through the roof. But I like those nails. Sometimes there's meaning in things that isn't obvious. Sometimes pain is necessary to teach a lesson. Sometimes lessons are being taught that we feel, even if we don't understand.

Kathy has cancer. Like all of us, she is dying, but for her, dying is very real. Thankfully, Kathy is a woman of tremendous faith. Recently she told me that since she's been diagnosed with cancer all sorts of wonderful things have happened. She's received cards and letters from people she hasn't seen in many years. Her children have become more responsive, and her estranged brother called to say he loved her. Kathy believes that every dark cloud has a silver lining. Having cancer is bad, but it ushers in many blessings if you choose to look at the bright side.

I got my driver's license the day I turned sixteen. I had been driving for years, so I was pretty comfortable behind the wheel. About a week after I got my license, I was driving about twenty-five miles an hour on a snow-covered, icy country road. The car fishtailed and slid into a ditch. I tried to get out by accelerating as I shifted between forward and reverse. I was spinning my wheels, but the car wouldn't move. The more I tried, the more the wheels spun and seemed to slide deeper into the ditch. I was going nowhere. It was cold and getting dark, and I was scared. Then, from out of nowhere, an old man appeared. He lived in a house near the road, hidden from view. He must have heard my engine revving and my wheels spinning. I was startled when he tapped on the window, but I gladly accepted his offer to help.

"Mind if I get behind the wheel?" he asked.

"Sure. Thanks." I said softly. I was desperate. I climbed out as he got into the driver's seat. He put the car in low gear and gently began to let out the clutch as he barely touched the gas. The engine hardly spun above an idle, and ever so slowly my car inched forward, out of the icy hole I had dug, and back up onto the pavement. Like the old man pointing at the moon in the proverb, this old man showed me a valuable lesson: *It's easier to get traction when you slow down.*

We all get stuck, figuratively and literally. Sometimes we go from one ditch to another, getting stuck, and then getting stuck even worse. When we're sliding and spinning, we tend to forget the simple solution for getting unstuck. We go faster, thinking that it will help, but going faster lands us deeper in the ditch. We're not stupid, but we tend to be stubborn.

One day recently while I was editing this manuscript, I decided to bake cookies. I set the timer in the kitchen and retreated to my office to continue editing. If you put your nose close to the page, you can almost smell the aroma of burned cookies. Let that smell be a reminder of what I learned that day: *Going too fast, multitasking, is a recipe for failure.*

At Pecos Benedictine Monastery in New Mexico, there's a monk named John. Brother John is old and moves very slowly. When pilgrims come to the monastery they often observe Brother John walking at a snail's pace about the grounds. During retreats, Brother John teaches what he calls a meditative walk. The walk involves a simple mantra, repeated at slow speed, while carefully placing one foot in front of the other. If you can imagine a foot race, now imagine the opposite. The goal is to walk as slowly as you can without stopping or falling. While you "walk" you repeat an inspirational phrase. After about twenty minutes, even though you haven't covered much physical ground, your mind can circle the globe. Meditative walking (and other intentionally slow activities) relax your body and refresh your mind.

Exercise 8

Today is a perfect day to begin the rest of
your life's journey. If you are determined to
accomplish much, if you truly want to make
a difference, put down your cell phone, turn
off all your electronic devices and go outside.
Find a quiet spot. Try Brother John's walking
meditation, sit, or stand quietly and breathe.
Your mind will be flooded with thoughts at
first, but allow them to drift away until you
are alone, at peace with yourself in nature.
Don't forget a few minutes for your listening
exercise. When you are completely relaxed,
close your eyes, listen, and let your mind see
the world in a new light.

Thought for the Day:
The faster I go, the more I fall behind.

CHAPTER NINE

Baseball and Bad Habits

Pete was the greatest hitter of his generation. His nickname was Charlie Hustle. Maybe it was because they called him Charlie, or maybe it was because he played with such enthusiasm, but for whatever reason, he was my baseball hero. Yet despite his on field accomplishments, Pete is not enshrined in the Baseball Hall of Fame.

Pete bet on baseball games (and many other things that people bet on). In an interview he once explained that he substituted the rush of gambling for the rush of playing baseball. He craved competition, and when he could no longer play his sport, he substituted the excitement of gambling. He lives in Las Vegas, spends time at casinos, gets paid to sign autographs for fans, and will most likely go to his grave without Hall of Fame recognition. Most would consider his love of gambling a stupid mistake.

In a recent interview, Pete admitted that he loves to bet, even though he understands that his gambling habit is keeping him out of the Baseball Hall of Fame. The commissioner of Major League Baseball told Pete that if he changed his lifestyle, baseball might consider lifting the lifetime ban that keeps him away from the game and out of the Hall of Fame. But Pete, despite a little voice that surely tells him not to, continues to gamble. He has chosen the path of punishment over that of reward. He knew he shouldn't bet on baseball games, but he did it anyway.

He knows he should trade gambling for behavior more acceptable to the commissioner and Hall of Fame voters, but despite knowing the preferred course of action, he continues on his chosen course of action.

Barry was the most prolific home run hitter of all time, and yet, like Pete, Barry is not in the Baseball Hall of Fame either. Everyone who ever saw Barry play agrees that his talents and performance before the steroid period of baseball would have been sufficient to land him a spot in the Hall of Fame. Unfortunately for Barry, his association with steroids left an indelible mark on his reputation. His choice to bulk up will also keep him out of the Hall of Fame. So why did Pete and Barry, both shoo-in Hall of Famers, choose actions that will forever tarnish their reputations? Why do you and I continue to do things that threaten our own well-being? What makes intelligent, talented people choose to go against their inner compass and rush headlong into disastrous decisions?

There are people in every walk of life who have made choices that haunt them. Some have lost fame and fortune, others have lost their lives, living on the edge, pushing the limits, and convincing themselves that it was OK, when in their hearts they knew it wasn't. There's a fine line between addiction and repeating bad decisions. Whatever the cause, the solution begins with awareness and a conscious decision to modify our behavior.

Burning your finger is usually a stupid mistake. When we are children, sooner or later we learn hot. Mom or dad says, "Don't touch that, it's hot." Invariably, we touch something hot and feel a little pain. From that point forward, we know and understand hot. Although we still burn our fingers from time to time, we have all become proficient at avoiding touching things that are hot. Other than in a magic trick, it is hard to imagine someone intentionally placing a hand in fire. Hot is a lesson that's easily learned and seldom forgotten.

Unfortunately, and unlike your stove, our stupid mistake zone isn't lined with glowing red burners. We don't always pay attention. Even though we recognize stupid mistakes, we continue to get burned. Getting burned isn't always accompanied by blistered skin and immediate pain. Getting burned doesn't always involve putting your finger in hot wax or on a pan you just took out of the oven. Sometimes we don't even feel the pain of our stupid mistakes. Some stupid mistakes only hurt other people. If we can learn hot, why do we continue to repeat our other stupid mistakes?

I'm only qualified to speak for myself. The stupid mistakes I repeat are caused by my failure to be mindful. When I'm thinking about something other than baking cookies, for example, I'm more likely to put my hand on a hot surface. When I'm not paying attention during a conversation, I'm more likely to say something that comes off as harsh or insensitive. Being mindful, paying attention, staying focused and living in the moment are the best cures for repeat stupid mistakes.

If you are a person who has become trapped by one stupid mistake that repeats itself, it's time for a look in the mirror. If you know it's wrong, why do you do it? Why don't you take steps to rid your life of that particular problem and start being the person you want to be? Can you muster the courage to step away from your obsession long enough to think about what it's doing to you and the people around you? Are you willing to face the consequences of owning your bad behavior? Are you ready to get serious about your issues? If you can't break your stupid mistake cycle alone, get help. There are lots of professionals trained to deal with your specific problem.

Exercise 9

Your listening exercise today is designed to help you find patterns. Listen for sounds that repeat themselves. The sound may be near or far away. It may be interrupted by a louder sound, but once you identify a repeating sound, focus on that sound and stick with it. Identify what it is and concentrate on the way it repeats itself.

Thought for the Day:
You get to choose: Hall of Fame or Hall of Shame.

CHAPTER TEN

Help From A Stranger

I never got his name. I met him only once, briefly. He spoke Spanish so I only understood a portion of what he said, but he taught me a lesson I will never forget. We met in San Antonio Abad, a beautiful little port city on the island of Ibiza, ninety miles southeast of Barcelona in the Mediterranean Sea. In 1976, I moved to Ibiza to contemplate the next chapter of life and write a book (not this one). We were living off savings and making every dollar stretch as far as possible. When the money was gone it would be time to head back to work in the salt mine. (My salt mine was a radio station in San Francisco, but when you're living the life on a Mediterranean island any real job seems like a salt mine.)

It was a weekday, and the town was fairly quiet. I stepped out of my little Spanish car and up onto the sidewalk. Right in front of me was a wad of money. It was just laying there. It was almost as big as a softball, tied with rubber bands. As I bent over to pick it up, I looked around and saw that the sidewalk was empty. It was obviously a considerable sum of money. I peeled back a few large bills and determined that it was someone's savings, maybe their life savings. My five year old son was anxious to get to wherever we were headed that day, but I explained that we had to wait. We leaned against a building and watched as a few people walked by, coming and going along the narrow street. It wasn't long before I spotted him. A middle-aged man, about a block away, with a look of panic that was unmistakable. He was walking in jerks and starts, his head on a swivel, looking everywhere from the sidewalk to the curb. He had a wild look in his eyes, and I knew in an instant that the small fortune I held belonged to him. As he approached, I walked toward him, smiled, and handed him his savings. It was a moment that I will remember forever.

The stranger, overcome with joy, shouted and jumped up and down. He tried to hand me some of the money. When I refused he hugged me and he hugged my son. He was so excited and talking so fast I couldn't understand half the words, but his meaning was clear. He had made a stupid mistake and dropped his fortune on the sidewalk. It was my good fortune to undo his stupid mistake. The impact of that event was so strong that it has survived for many years. Even today, I can recall the emotional rush I had that day. It's one of the most memorable days of my life.

For an instant, when I first reached down to pick up the stranger's money, I considered what would have been a stupid mistake. It would have been extremely easy to slip the money into my pocket and continue on down the street. My son wouldn't have noticed or would have soon forgotten. There was nobody near us at that moment, and no one saw me pick it up. God knows I could have used the money. But in that instant, my little voice prevailed. I avoided a stupid mistake and decided to do the right thing.

There are hundreds of opportunities each year to do the right thing. Not every situation is as dramatic as the one I experienced in Ibiza, but we all have random moments when we can help a stranger. You don't have to go around looking for lost treasures to return to their rightful owner. Sometimes it is as easy as a smile. When someone cuts you off in traffic and you pull up next to him at the next stop light, the stupid mistake is to make an angry gesture or shout through your open window. Sometimes helping a stranger is as easy as saying, "Have a nice day."

Recently I was backing out of a parking space when a car approached with horn blaring. I immediately hit the brakes. Since

I was completely out of the parking spot, and as soon as I was sure the approaching car had stopped, I continued pulling out. As we passed, heading in opposite directions, I saw that the driver was an elderly woman. She had apparently been startled by my exit and appeared a bit embarrassed by blasting her horn at me. As I made eye contact, I gave her my biggest smile and waved as if I knew her. What could she do? She smiled back, and we continued on our journeys, more aware of traffic and our own reactions to unexpected obstacles.

There are thousands of stories about stupid mistakes with tragic endings. We all know about people who took what didn't belong to them or became involved in road rage. But there are millions of untold stories about kindness and awareness. People are naturally programmed to help other people. Extreme selfishness is a learned behavior. Think of all the times that others have lifted you up. Remember the times when you were down in the dumps and someone did something so amazingly kind that it brought an immediate smile. When you're having a bad day and nothing is going your way, break the spell with a kind thought, word or gesture directed at a stranger. Sometimes people will pass by quickly, wondering why you smiled or waived at them, but somewhere down the line, it will come back to them. The world gets nicer one gesture at a time.

In our neighborhood, and in other neighborhoods where I've lived over the years, I wave at people. If I'm driving and they're walking (lots of folks walk their dogs in my neighborhood), I wave. If I'm walking (alone or with my dog) I wave at the people passing in their cars. In rural communities and small towns, this used to be an American custom. When you pass someone, you wave. Wave when you see someone walking or riding a bike, driving a car or a golf cart. Wave to acknowledge them as human beings and as neighbors. It's still a custom in many parts of the world, but we've become increasingly isolated from our neighbors and the practice of waving has diminished. Try it. You'll be pleasantly surprised. Some people will drive past without acknowledgment. Some will give you a strange look. But some will wave back. You'll have connected with other people who are also paying attention and trying to do the right thing.

Exercise 10

Your listening exercise today is social. Find a spot where there are people milling about. Close your eyes and listen. Hear their voices. Try to notice if there's music or if anyone is singing. Enjoy your place in the crowd. Sit quietly and just listen to the human condition. You'll find that it's not that bad.

Thought for the Day:
A stranger can become your best friend, but it won't happen unless you say or do something friendly.

CHAPTER ELEVEN

Fantastic and Beautiful

Asking friends about their one stupid mistake has become an exercise in understanding. One friend said, "I brought my wife a cheeseburger without bacon." Another said, "I should never have started my own company. I should have gone to work for a big company so I could sleep at night." Each person has his or her own version of one stupid mistake. Some are simple, some are complex, but they are always connected to regret.

When we learn to do the right thing for the right reason, and practice daily, we develop immunity against disappointment. Life might not always go our way, but each day we celebrate more victories than defeats as we practice living a purposeful life.

Woody worked at a radio station in San Francisco. He wasn't especially talented. He read copy and sounded like an announcer, but he wasn't what you'd call a creative guy. He did his job, followed directions, and that was about it. Every day he slogged through life doing his best, which wasn't especially good. He kept his head down, and his nose to the grindstone. But Woody had a magic phrase. When anyone asked him how his day was going, Woody always replied: "Fantastic." He didn't color it with other words or phrases, he simply replied "Fantastic." One day I asked Woody why he always answered that way and he explained. "If you're feeling sad, disappointed, or sick, they don't really want to know. They're just being polite. It doesn't help anything by bringing them down, so I just say what makes them feel better." Woody paused. "And nine times out of ten, I feel better too after I say it," he told me. We could always count on Woody to make us feel better, because no matter how his day was going, Woody was fantastic.

My friend Mike used a different response to the same question. Mike would say "beautiful." He was a big, burly guy who worked with his hands, so hearing him say "beautiful" in his deep manly voice always made me smile. Like Woody, even if he was having a horrible day, if you asked Mike how he was doing, he'd smile and brighten your day.

Each time we speak we have a decision to make. We choose between bringing the world up or down to our level. Every word is a choice. It's stupid to say negative things. What good does it accomplish to share anger, frustration, disappointment or despair? You might say it makes you feel better, but we know that's not true. Thinking negative thoughts and saying negative words always have the same effect, and it's never good. Have you ever considered that your words take on an external life of their own? When you say something, the meaning of your words is transferred to the receiver. Everyone is aware of the simple idea of "paying it forward." Why not practice by choosing words (and repeating them often) that lift others? Fantastic and beautiful are simple greetings that make people feel better. Making somebody feel better is always a good decision.

When we learned cursive writing in school, we also learned letter writing etiquette. The template I learned had the salutation "dear" at the beginning of the letter, and the word "sincerely" as the closing (before the signature). Today people use words like "best" or "regards"; sometimes they don't write anything and simply sign their names. When's the last time you got a letter or email signed "sincerely?" Are we less sincere today than when I learned to write? Can you think of other uplifting words that have disappeared from common usage? Break out a few and experiment with them. Watch how people react when you smile and share a friendly word. Even if you feel crappy, spread some cheer. Guarantee it will lighten your load.

Exercise 11

Your listening exercise today has to do with high and low. Listen for the high sounds. High pitched sounds are good for starters, but try to hear a sound that's coming from overhead. Can you hear a bird singing high in a tree? Is there a plane flying high above? Concentrate on lifting your awareness to a higher level. Stay at it till you feel fantastic!

Thought for the Day:
Choose uplifting words. They work both ways.

CHAPTER TWELVE

Stupid Mistakes in a Bottle

David forgot his pajamas. A rear admiral in the U.S. Navy, David was on a business trip at an important conference. After the day's business meeting, he enjoyed a cocktail with associates and a glass of wine at dinner. The alcohol reacted poorly with David's blood pressure medication, so, feeling a little tipsy, he retreated to his room. Later that night, the admiral got up to go to the bathroom, but instead of stepping into the bathroom, he stepped into the hallway. When the door closed behind him, he was naked.

Hotel hallways are a bad place to be naked. Guests at the hotel including two women saw him "out of uniform" and complained to hotel security. As fate would have it, the security guard arrived without a master key. David and the guard had to ride the elevator together, and a hotel elevator is also a bad place to be naked. At the front desk they found a towel and a key, but the damage was done. David was court-martialed for conduct unbecoming an officer. Any one of the admiral's mistakes might have been forgiven, but combined, they cost him his job.

When you forget to pack pajamas, forget that your medications don't mix well with alcohol, and forget to put the chain lock on your hotel room door you've made three small mistakes. Even small mistakes can cause a lifetime of embarrassment. David's picture (in uniform) still appears when you Google "naked admiral."

Ed was a big man, well over six feet and two hundred pounds. My dad was small, five-six, and less than a hundred fifty pounds. Ed came into our grocery store shouting. He was slurring his words and it was obvious that he was drunk. My dad, who was dead sober and very annoyed, told Ed to leave. Ed continued to shout and came at my father. I feared for my dad's life, but then Dad hit him with a left-right combination, and the much bigger man went sprawling to the floor. It all happened in an instant. Neighbors who were in the store helped Ed to his feet and took him home. The next day, when he sobered up, Ed came in and apologized to my dad. Childhood memories leave lasting impressions. Drunk people make stupid mistakes.

Before we moved to the grocery store, we lived in the back of a tavern. I saw lots of drunks when I was a kid. Before I went to sleep at night I often wandered into the bar in my pajamas to say goodnight to my dad and mom who were tending bar. Some of my first memories are of people reeking of alcohol and slurring their words. As disgusting as that sounds, I wonder if my parents knew that exposing me to drunks at an early age would help create a permanent distaste for drunks. It worked. Although I've had one too many on occasion over the years, I don't like being drunk and I don't like being around drunks.

When we moved from the tavern to the store, we obviously didn't escape the environment. In the small rural community where we lived, we were never very far from drinking and drunks. Across the highway from the store was another small tavern. In the summertime we were allowed to stay out till nine or ten. Neighborhood kids hid in the bushes behind that tavern to watch local drunks fight one another on Friday and Saturday night.

After a long day of drinking, at least a couple local rowdies would get into an argument, and eventually it would spill out into the back parking lot. They'd swear, slip, slide and occasionally land a punch or two. The next day, they sobered up and forgot what happened. They were back at the same bar to drink with the same people. Getting drunk and getting into a fight was just routine behavior.

I'm quite certain you've never seen the kind of Friday night fights we saw. You likely never saw your father knock a man down with his fists. But I'll bet you have seen someone stumbling after too much to drink. I'll bet you have heard a person slurring words. In fact, if you're an adult in America, it's almost guaranteed that you've seen an obnoxious drunk doing something totally stupid. The question is: Are you that person? How many times have you made the personal connection between drinking and stupid mistakes?

Alcohol has been linked to life-changing mistakes for centuries. Lives and careers are regularly sacrificed to the bottle. Alcohol kills those who drink to excess as well as scores of innocent bystanders. Millions of deaths and scarred psyches are directly attributed to over-consumption. Drunk people say and do stupid things. Drunk people make terrible parents. Anyone could write a paragraph for this chapter. Either you, or someone you know, or someone you have seen has been what we call "stupid drunk."

Even though it's well documented that every time we drink too much we make bad decisions, some of you don't remember your drunken mistakes, much less learn from them. Despite the facts, Americans continue to consume record amounts of alcohol. My home state of Wisconsin used to hold the national per capita record for alcohol consumption, but Nevada now claims that title.

Some drunks are happy, some are sad, and some are mean. We laugh at happy drunks, but when they wake up the next day they aren't happy. We feel pity for sad drunks crying in their beer. If we're sober, we find them pathetic. When we're drinking with them, we become depressed with them. Mean drunks are the worst, though. They pick fights and try to hurt people. Drinking helps them mask their problems. They blame others and become angry. Mean drunks abuse their spouses and children. Mean drunks get in cars and trucks and drive aggressively. Mean drunks injure and kill innocents.

Alcoholism is a disease. If you are addicted, you may need professional help to quit drinking. My dad was an alcoholic and a chain smoker. When he had children he quit drinking. A few years later he quit smoking. He was a strong-willed person, and he did both without professional help. He quit both drinking and smoking cold turkey. That's it, that's enough, I quit. People with strong wills can beat addictive behavior. My dad never taught me how to fight, but he taught me self-control. I learned that I am responsible for my actions.

If you choose, you can stop drinking. You can also stop smoking, stop gambling, stop overeating and stop making stupid mistakes. It may not be easy, but it has been done, and you can do it.

Just because everybody else is doing it (whatever it is), you don't have to follow the crowd. You don't have to drink socially to have a good time or fit in.

I once had a mean boss who used alcohol as a weapon against her employees. She prided herself on her ability to hold her liquor. During a night on the town, she plied subordinates (mostly men) with alcohol, and coaxed them to say things she could use against them later. She was ruthless. When I first went to work for her, a friend warned me about how she operated. I remembered a story my dad told me about how to get a leg up on a drunk.

I was too young to drink when he told me, but I tried it at a business meeting in Philadelphia. I arrived at the restaurant a half hour before our meeting. I found the bartender that was working all evening, and I handed him twenty dollars. I instructed him to make my drinks without alcohol. I'd order vodka and tonic, but he'd serve me tonic water. I promised to tip him again after dinner. He charged for vodka and tonic, but there was no vodka in my drinks.

That may have been my favorite meeting. While she and my colleagues were drinking all night and getting plastered, I was laughing and having a great time. I watched her set traps, and never let on that I was cold sober. The next day everyone suffered; everyone but me. (I hope she reads this.)

If you regularly drink too much or have a drink every day, you may have a drinking problem. You make excuses for your behavior. You convince yourself that you're simply a social drinker or that a drink or two helps you relax. You might tell yourself that you could quit if you wanted to, but you don't want to. If alcohol has been a part of your routine for a long time, it's hard to imagine a day without a drink or two. Some drunks, often after an embarrassing incident, outgrow the behavior. They do something so stupid and so destructive that they finally face reality and quit drinking.

Drug abuse is equally destructive. In fact, drug abuse is fast approaching alcohol abuse on the stupid chart. Each of us knows someone who died from a drug overdose. Stop and think about that statement. Each of us knows someone who died from a drug overdose. You're reading this book because you're looking for answers. Here's an answer: Drug abuse is a stupid mistake. If you use recreational drugs or prescribed drugs in a manner that goes beyond your doctor's recommendation, you have a problem. Addiction sucks. Ask any addict. Don't wait till your problem grows beyond your control. Don't pretend that you can manage the problem. If you rely on drugs to get through the day or to get to sleep every night, get help.

Tom is a trainer at my gym. He's also an alcoholic. He told me that working out everyday has replaced his dependence on alcohol and drugs. If Tom can do it, so can you.

Exercise 12

Your listening exercise today is very simple. Find a quiet place. Close your eyes. Concentrate on every sound as you work yourself further and further away from where you are. The ability to stay with this listening exercise is strengthening your willpower. You are moving ever closer to conscious awareness. You are shedding stupid mistakes. Keep listening.

Thought for the Day:
Lives are ruined by stupid drinking and drug abuse. Is it really worth it?

CHAPTER THIRTEEN

The Tie that Binds

Al was a well known radio news anchor in San Francisco. He was a quiet, dignified, soft-spoken professional man with a great voice. He was considerate to a fault, and I never heard him speak an unkind word. One day Al approached me and complimented me on my tie. Immediately, as has been my practice for many years, I took off the tie, handed it to him and said, "It's yours."

Al was a bit uncomfortable at first, but when he realized that I was pleased to give him a gift, he graciously accepted. After that, for the seven years we worked together Al wore that tie at least once a week. One tie, once a week, seven years. The tie created a special connection. He'd wear the tie, and I'd compliment him by saying "nice tie." He'd ask if I wanted it back, and I'd tell him that it looked much better on him. That was our routine for seven years. The same exchange always ended with a good laugh.

Of all the ties I've given away, none had as much impact. I've often wondered if Al really liked the tie or if he was just being polite by wearing it so often. Al was an enormously nice man and he regularly did kind things to make other people feel better, so it wouldn't surprise me to learn that he didn't even like the tie that much. He lived a long, happy and productive life. When he died, hundreds of people were grateful for the opportunity to have known him. Thousands more mourned the loss of a great person.

The biggest single stupid mistake we can make is to think we are the most important person in our world. Seriously. How many times have you charged ahead with your plan of action, only to find that nobody is following? People who put themselves first, ahead of everyone else, create the illusion that their thoughts, words and actions are most important. That's an illusion. It's also a stupid mistake.

The best way to connect is to pay attention to others. "Taking care of number one" is a popular saying, and it's also what's wrong with the world. Narcissism is ugly. Falling in love with your ideas and your self-image won't take you where you want to go. My mother had a habit of speaking bluntly (after all, she spent many years tending bar), and sometimes her vocabulary was a bit "salty". One of mom's sayings was, "Don't get carried away with your own bullshit." If you can get past the image of my mother using the "bs" word, the meaning rings as true today as when I first heard her say it.

Try this experiment (and I'm guessing some of you have already done this): Go out and buy whatever you want. If you have the money, buy anything that "your heart desires." You will find, for a short while, that there is great pleasure in your purchase. You can show your friends and show off what you have. After a very short while, however, the novelty of your purchase wears off, and it's just another thing. If you can afford it, go out and purchase something else. After a series of unnecessary purchases you'll come to realize that buying things for yourself fails to create lasting happiness. Getting things brings us pleasure, but pleasure is fleeting. Giving a gift that's appreciated by another, however, gives us joy, and joy lasts forever.

You've heard the expression many times, "There is more joy in giving than receiving." That bit of wisdom holds true for more than physical possessions. A smile, a friendly wave, a kind word or a compliment can make someone's day. And unlike buying something you don't need, every time you lift spirits you get a warm feeling that stays with you. Long after the moment has passed, you are likely to remember it. And when you do, that same fulfilling feeling washes over you anew. When you put the emphasis on another person, when you watch and listen carefully and attend to their needs, you are most unlikely to make stupid mistakes.

We all have friends and family who can't seem to control themselves. They may be emotionally immature. They don't feel good about themselves, so they overcompensate by being loud, brash, self-centered or arrogant. Generally speaking, people who live that way end up lonely and alone. When you think about someone like that, even though you love them, you wish they could see the shallow nature of their false bravado. If that profile fits you, and you find yourself talking more than listening, judging others more often than you reflect on your own flaws, pushing to the front of the line or dressing in a way that is sure to be noticed, maybe this chapter is for you.

There's a parable that suggests the first will be last and the last will be first. In it, a person attends a wedding feast and sits way down at the wrong end of the guest table. The person throwing the party goes down and takes him to a seat of greater honor. He is rewarded for his humility, while another guest who pushes to the front and sits near the wedding party is embarrassed when the host asks him to move down and make way for a more important guest. It's a life lesson too often lost on members of the Me Generation.

There are two types of people—givers and takers. While there is nothing wrong with graciously accepting a gift or favor from another, there truly is more joy in giving.

Exercise 13

Your daily listening exercise involves getting and staying outside yourself. Notice that when you close your eyes and start listening, every sound you hear comes from beyond your body. Start close and work your way to the furthest sound you can hear. Enjoy listening. There's a big world out there. It was there even before you started listening. It will be there even when you stop listening. Try to hear more clearly.

Thought for the Day:
Empathy reinforces our values by focusing on the values of others.

CHAPTER FOURTEEN

Don't Be Afraid to Try

Years ago I was in Atlantic City, New Jersey to accept a National Headliners Award on behalf of our news team. The night before the awards ceremony, never having been there before, I went for a walk down the boardwalk.

With fifty dollars in my pocket, I walked in and out of a couple of casinos. The tables were packed. I was hoping to find a five dollar game of craps or a dollar roulette wheel so I could people-watch for awhile before "donating" my stash to the house. (Like I said, I had never been to Atlantic City before!)

Casinos are great for people-watching, because most of the people gambling are so absorbed in their game that they don't notice people watching them. I was weaving my way along when I came upon a craps table that was packed. There was a lot of excitement. It was a twenty-five dollar table, too rich for my blood.

The guy throwing the dice was new to the game and he was betting twenty-five dollars on the pass line. (Experienced players make multiple bets on each roll.) He was a big muscular guy with his shirt unbuttoned to display a large gold chain. As he received the dice he bragged to his girlfriend that the game was easy. "Like throwing a softball," he bellowed as his exaggerated underhand motion bounced the dice off the other end of the table.

Despite his obvious lack of knowledge of the game, he was on a lucky streak the likes of which I had never seen. He threw seven and eleven on his opening rolls, and when he was throwing for a point, he mesmerized the assembled crowd by throwing number after number without crapping out before finally throwing a winner.

Craps is a somewhat complicated game with a variety of bets. You can bet with the person throwing the dice, or you can bet against him. You can bet on individual numbers or combinations of numbers, and as with most casino games, the more you bet, the more you win or lose. If you throw seven or eleven on your first roll you win the pass line bet. If you throw two, three or twelve (craps) you lose. If you throw a number between four and eleven (other than seven) that becomes your "point" or target. You keep throwing until you either "make your point" or throw a seven that ends your turn.

As I wedged my way in close to the table, I found myself standing behind an old man. As I've come to learn over the years, old men frequently know quite a bit about craps and life. The old man was betting on the pass line, taking odds behind the line, and betting all the numbers. When he won on a number, he pressed (doubled) his bet. If he won again, he used his winnings to double his bet yet again. Meanwhile the guy with the dice couldn't miss. He'd throw a number and every one of the old man's numbers, and then he'd throw a winner and do it again. I stood there watching the old man rake in pile after pile of black one hundred dollar chips. He had several hundred dollars on the table for every roll, and each time the big guy won $25 the old man won a thousand dollars or more.

A craps table has built-in trays all around the top edge for players' chips, and every row of the old man's trays was full of black chips. He had a large bucket under the table, and that too was full of chips. At one point his wife came to the table but he gruffly shooed her away. He was so totally into the game that he didn't want to be bothered. She thought better of saying something to him when she saw his stash of chips. He was winning more money than I could imagine.

After a couple minutes I considered putting my fifty dollars on the pass line next to the old man's bet, but I was afraid. I feared losing fifty dollars, and even more I feared the wrath of the old man if my bet somehow jinxed the table. Winner after winner, I heard my little voice say "put your money on the line you chicken," but I kept my money in my pocket and the old man continued stacking hundred dollar chips. I watched this spectacle for at least a half hour.

A half hour is an eternity in the life of a craps shooter. The guy with the dice was winning. Yet because he didn't understand the game and never increased his bet, he only won twenty-five dollars at a time. The old man, on the other hand, was literally winning thousands. The stupid guy named Charlie standing behind the old man wagered nothing and won nothing.

Fear of failure leads to stupid mistakes. While I left with the same fifty dollars, when it was over, I knew that I had missed an opportunity. I don't often go to casinos, but when I do, I either win a little or lose a little. The type of run I witnessed that night is the stuff of legends. My fifty dollars could easily have turned to hundreds or even thousands. Fear of losing fifty dollars prevented me from making a small fortune.

I'm sharing the story because I've since come to realize that it's an metaphor for life. You can't win if you don't play the game.

My dad died a poor man. He once told me that his employer offered him a small island in exchange for wages. The pay he was due for working in the woods during the winter was less than two hundred dollars. (Mind you, in today's dollars that would be several thousand dollars, but he told me the story to make a point.) He turned down the small island located in the backwaters of the Wisconsin River because there was no bridge to the island. In order to get to the island, you had to cross about twenty feet of water. He passed on taking title to the island and held out for a little less than two hundred dollars cash.

Today that island has a dozen million dollar plus homes. The small bridge to the island was built seventy-five years ago and is hardly noticeable when you pass from the mainland into this semi-exclusive neighborhood.

How many times have you witnessed life happening in front of you? How many times have you lacked the courage to take a chance on what appeared to be a sure thing? Did you pass on the opportunity to invest in a new stock that became Google or Amazon? Have you ever seen a special person that you felt you should meet and then let the moment pass without introducing yourself? Do you wonder what could have been if you had pursued another course of action?

When life passes us by, there's no going back. We can't change the past. What's done is done. It doesn't help to carry regrets for actions not taken. Stupid mistakes are ones we make against our better judgement. Sometimes that involves acting, and sometimes it involves not acting. Fear is a bad companion. Fear drowns out your little voice. When your little voice tells you to take a chance, take a chance. If you feel like you have a connection, push through your shyness and say hello to a stranger. Consider the situation and take prudent chances. That doesn't mean your life savings belong in a casino or the stock market, but sometimes it's important to take reasonable chances.

When we get to be old men and old women, we're bound to have a few regrets. We're bound to have made stupid mistakes and missed certain opportunities. Today's reflection is a reminder that doing nothing, taking the safest path, isn't always the right choice.

Exercise 14

Your listening exercise involves staying with one sound and counting. Is it a clock? A hammer in the distance? A special bird? Listen and softly count as the sound repeats itself. Each repetition represents an opportunity. During your short listening exercise you'll be counting opportunities.

Thought for the Day:
You can't win the prize if you don't enter the contest.

CHAPTER FIFTEEN

Taking a Second Chance Again

Bill Gates's first business failed. Stephen King's first novel was rejected thirty times. Oprah Winfrey was fired from her first TV job. Katy Perry's first album was a flop. Before he became an icon, Henry Ford founded the Detroit Automobile Company and drove it into bankruptcy. He had to walk away from his second company too. It wasn't until his third try that he founded the Ford Motor Company. We're told that Thomas Edison tried ten thousand failed experiments before he successfully invented the electric light bulb. Walt Disney was once fired from a newspaper job because he lacked imagination. Get the picture?

What if any of these or the millions of other successful people in the world would have quit after a personal failure? Quitting is a stupid mistake. As important as it is to learn from our mistakes, it is equally important not to give up because we failed on our first attempt. When NASA scientists consider their faulty calculations on the first attempts to boost a capsule beyond the atmosphere, or Hall of Fame athletes look back on their rookie seasons, they laugh at how misguided they were back in the day. Trial and error is a basic component of success. It doesn't matter how many times it takes, getting it right is the correct thing to do.

We are confused by failure. We gave it our best shot (or so we think), it didn't work out, so what's the point in trying again? Whether driven by ego, fear of failure, or just lack of faith, one and done is a common stupid mistake.

Remember earlier we talked about doing the same thing with the same circumstances and expecting a different result? That's insanity. But taking another bite at the apple is the approach that separates winners from losers. Nearly every successful business person in America can tell a story about a previous failure. Disappointment is never easy to swallow, but drive and determination to succeed are critical. Trying and failing allows successful people to learn from their mistakes. "Let's try that again" isn't limited to being successful in business. Millions of happy people failed at relationships before finding success.

The tragedy of suicide is related to the mistaken notion that there's no hope for a better outcome. Shakespeare's *Romeo and Juliet* epitomizes the futility of failing to consider all the options. Sometimes our stupid mistakes seem irreparable. Sometimes it feels like nobody could ever understand our suffering. Failure is a hard pill to swallow. Unless you put things in perspective, every failure, every stupid mistake seems to spell doom.

The truth is, even the happiest most successful people on earth experience sadness, disappointment and defeat. Baseball players who made an out seven out of ten times are regularly inducted into the Baseball Hall of Fame. In sports we understand that "you can't win 'em all." It's the same in life. Great champions don't win every game or match. Great writers don't write bestsellers every time out. Great thinkers don't always solve the problem. *Sometimes you win, sometimes you lose, but there is no loss so overpowering that doesn't merit a second chance.*

Married couples that have been together for over fifty years didn't experience sunshine and roses every day. I've talked to many couples who admit that there were times when they feared that their relationship was on the rocks. Life isn't easy. Living with another person brings a whole new set of challenges. The difference between many couples who are divorced and those that stay together boils down to effort. One of the phrases from our past that is lost on many modern Americans should be posted on more refrigerators: "When the going gets tough, the tough get going." It's a clever phrase that captures the essence of second and third effort. True, there may come a time when you throw in the towel and say enough is enough, but if you haven't done everything in your power to make it work, you should try again.

I know people who say they'll never fall in love again because the first attempt didn't work out the way they hoped. Some refuse to fly because they experienced a turbulent flight or a bumpy landing. Fred tried sushi one time and has since sworn off all Asian food. Alison won't go to a concert because she once got caught in a crowd and was frightened. Sylvia refuses to drive on a freeway after witnessing an accident. Whatever the situation, giving up because you tried, failed (or got scared) is stupid. Giving up may be easy, but it isn't your best idea. It's up to you to determine if the glass is half full or half empty. It's OK if you choose not to fly or decide that you don't like sushi, but limiting your options simply because of one bad experience eventually becomes a stupid mistake.

I jumped out of an airplane once. I haven't skydived since, but I know if I had to, I could do it. It scared me, but I survived. It was enjoyable, sort of, and I gained a great respect for people who regularly skydive. Played naked volleyball at a nudist colony, too. Same thing. Could do it again if I wanted to, but I haven't found myself in any nudist colonies recently. Overcoming fear and keeping an open mind are steps toward eliminating stupid mistakes. Disappointment and failed experiences are an essential part of the learning process. *Giving up is a stupid mistake that keeps many people from achieving their full potential.*

Exercise 15

Let's listen for seven to ten minutes and see if we can identify a sound we have never heard before. As you listen more closely, you might come to recognize it. Sometimes our mind sends us mixed signals and rejects things prematurely. We might think we don't know what we are hearing, but on second thought, we do know that sound.

Thought for the Day:
If at first you don't succeed, try, try again.

CHAPTER SIXTEEN

Einstein's Brother

Ronald is a theoretical physicist who is constructing a time machine. His father died at an early age. My dad passed away when I was 12, so I can relate to his story. He is driven to find a way to go back in time by a desire to save his father's life. As a young man he was fascinated with both fictional time travel and Einstein's theories of general relativity. When he was eight, he decided that he would conquer the bounds of time. His decision has led him to countless hours of study and a PhD in physics.

Einstein is famous for E=mc², but few understand what it means, and even fewer know the story associated with Einstein's discovery. In simplest terms, Einstein explained that energy is equal to mass times the constant speed of light squared. The theory states that the farther and faster you travel, the less impact time has on you. In movies, time travelers return to Earth after a long journey in space. They haven't aged much, but everyone left behind on earth is either very old or dead and gone. We imagine that this is one of the outcomes of prolonged space travel. A couple years ago, scientists used a super powerful telescope to prove that the theory is correct. When we figure out how to build a time machine, it will be possible to go back in time. Ronald believes that will be accomplished in this century.

So what does relativity and time travel have to do with decisions and stupid mistakes? Theoretically, if we could go back in time today, we could undo all the stupid mistakes that we've made. The world would be a better place.

Unfortunately, at this time, we don't have a time travel machine. Our technology can record every action and even predict with some certainty future actions, but we can't undo stupid mistakes once they've happened. The good news is that people who learn to avoid stupid mistakes by making good decisions, can live happier and better in the future.

Einstein was on to something, and how he got there is the reason we're heading down this rabbit hole. Where did Einstein get the idea? How did he begin to imagine the time-space continuum? Here's the story:

When Einstein was developing his famous theory of relativity, he imagined that he and his brother were racing on beams of light. Einstein was one second, or 186,000 miles ahead of his brother in this imaginary race. Einstein imagined that he would both send a signal to his brother and accelerate at the same time, so that by the time his brother received the signal to speed up, Einstein would maintain his lead. In other words, he'd signal his brother to speed up, but because he would hit his accelerator at the same time they would remain the same distance apart. He went to the blackboard and wrote it down and the famous E=mc2 (energy equals mass times the speed of light in a vacuum squared) changed the world. It led to the development of the atomic bomb and is considered one of the most important developments in theoretical physics.

The most incredible part of the story is that Einstein didn't even have a brother! He had a sister, but not a brother. In order to change the direction of the modern world, Einstein imagined a brother. What was to become his greatest scientific breakthrough was driven by the idea of two boys sitting on beams of light and having a race. He certainly could have envisioned a race against his sister, but for whatever reason, at the turn of the century no respectable young man would feel good about beating his little sister in a race!

Einstein knew that imagination is the key to creativity, and creativity brings beauty and progress. Inhibiting your own imagination or that of others is indeed a stupid mistake. Einstein endorsed and practiced this philosophy. While others were seeing the world as it is, he saw the world the way it could be. His genius was accompanied by an incredible sense of humor. He worked hard, but enjoyed having fun with friends and listening to music. Although he lived through a terrible period of history with much chaos and bloodshed, he regularly looked to the future and imagined positive outcomes.

That's the point. If one of the smartest people who ever lived used imagination and humor on a daily basis, why don't you? You may not be able to go back and fix all the mistakes you've made in the past, but you certainly can imagine a better life in your future. The world may be crazy and chaotic, but you can imagine brighter days in your future. Put your wishes to work for you. Imagination led Einstein to solve one of the great mysteries of the universe. It's a powerful tool, and it's as accessible to you as it was to Einstein.

Exercise 16

Your listening exercise today is to hear and
use your imagination at the same time. Listen
for those distant sounds and then imagine
them in an environment you create. If it's a
bird singing, imagine the tree where that bird
is perched. If it's a freight train, imagine the
engine and the cars on the train, what they look
like and where they are going. Whatever the
sound, imagine it in time and space. Focus on a
sound as you expand your worldview. Listen.

Thought for the Day:
*"Determination can take you many places, but
imagination can take you anywhere." —Albert
Einstein*

CHAPTER SEVENTEEN

Think Before You Speak

Susan has a tendency to say biting, sarcastic things, especially to members of her family and her closest friends. They have come to accept that it's Susan's defense mechanism to compensate for her self-esteem issues. Whenever someone gets too close for comfort, Susan lashes out with an unnerving comment about how they look, act, or speak. Her friends (the few that remain friends) have come to understand what's going on, but still find it difficult to keep their emotions under control when Susan is on the attack. Their first instinct is to greet fire with fire. But as they have learned, the worst thing you can do with such a person is respond in kind. Taking on an irrational person escalates the situation, and everyone in the room is then forced to cope with negative energy. Nothing good comes of people trading insults.

From time to time we all revert to unfiltered remarks. We blurt out what seems to us an obvious truth without regard for the impact of our words on others. When you speak before you think, you run the risk of seriously injuring the feelings of others. So what? Who cares if my words hurt? Screw 'em if they can't take it? Sometimes the truth hurts! These are just a few of the expressions we use to rationalize and justify hurtful behavior. Stupid mistakes originate in our brain, but many are executed with our mouth. Putting your foot in your mouth is an age old tradition. Putting your foot down someone's throat is barbaric.

A thoughtless word here, a careless tweet there, and before you know it you've dug a hole from which there is no escape.

There is one basic tenet of communication that should be your guiding principle: Before you say something that might hurt another, consider the situation, consider the audience, and determine whether your desire to blurt it out is more important than how your audience will react. Even if saying something for shock value may be consistent with your brand identity, for most people, a happy, peaceful life begins with courtesy and respect. You will reap what you sow. If you want people to treat you with sincerity, dignity, respect and compassion, it's imperative that you treat them the same way.

Recently, Susan made a snide remark about a friend's propensity to shower people with gifts for every occasion (and non-occasion). Instead of reacting emotionally, her friend smiled and explained that she enjoys giving gifts and hoped that her gifts didn't make others feel uncomfortable.

Greeting Susan's negativity with a positive, non-confrontational response was just the right medicine. Susan thought about it for a minute and then changed the subject. Your mouth is a dangerous weapon. While it has the potential to deliver compliments, praise and loving messages, it can cause irreparable damage to the human psyche. *We should have lip stickers that read, "Use With Caution."* Many stupid mistakes come when we're reacting to someone else's stupid comments. Emotional reaction to unpleasant words never has a positive outcome. Remember that we're all guilty at one time or another of saying inappropriate things. Even when you feel justified in your verbal counterpunch, it only exacerbates the problem. Harsh words in response to an insult is akin to extinguishing a fire with gasoline. Neither is likely to have the desired effect.

Exercise 17

Listen for the faintest sound. Listen for a sound beyond that sound. Hear the sounds of silence that lay well beyond the noise of the world. Lock in on that peaceful, quiet sound, the one that you have to strain to hear and stay with it for as long as you can. Emerge refreshed, renewed and committed to more focused thoughts, words and actions.

Thought for the Day:
Sticks and stones may break my bones, but mean-spirited, stupid words from others will not elicit an emotional response from me!

I Thought You Said

"What's that for?" asked the foreman.

"I thought you told me to bring it to you." replied the laborer.

The exasperated foreman replied, "I said let's take a break! Did you think I said bring me a rake?"

Do you ever daydream when someone is talking to you? Do you ever catch yourself thinking about something totally unrelated and then have to stumble back into a conversation? How many times have you walked away from a conversation in the wrong direction because you really weren't listening to what the other person was saying? Active listening is critical to communication and understanding, and with a thousand distractions all around us, it's not always easy to stay focussed on what is being communicated.

In preindustrial times, people gathered around the fire and listened as the tribe's designated storyteller shared oral history. Listening was just as important as speaking, and both the speaker and the listener took great pride in their roles. It was an honor to be able to listen. Before written communication, it was the only way information was disseminated. Unfortunately in our rush-around world, listening has become a lost art.

Active listening involves a conscious effort to understand exactly what another person is communicating. It requires eye contact and total concentration. Active listening includes awareness of body language, gestures, facial expressions, tone, inflection, and every element of oral language interpretation. Sometimes active listening requires taking notes—not doodling, but actually writing down keywords and phrases that will be helpful in capturing the essence of what's being said.

Remember my stupid lecture interruption from Chapter 2? You may have had a similar incident. You get excited to share something in conversation and you're so intent on what you have to say that you neglect to pay attention to the person speaking. You wait for the speaker to take a breath so you can jump in and insert your thought. Though your intentions may be good, the result is not. More often than not, interrupting a speaker spoils the moment for everybody involved.

Active listening requires setting aside your desire to shine. You'll get your chance to be brilliant and make a contribution, but not during the lecture. You can share your experience or a clever thought, but wait until the speaker has finished making a point. If you're intently listening, you'll know when it's appropriate to add to what is being said. If you're busy contemplating your next expression, you can't really be an active listener. If you're not paying attention to every word, phrase and sentence, you're not paying attention. If you're not paying attention, you're not an active listener. If you're not an active listener, your odds of saying or doing something stupid are magnified.

Pay attention. Stay in the moment. Meaningful communication demands that you listen attentively. Even when you have the urge to share a thought, when someone else is speaking it's your job to listen. Do your job.

Exercise 18

Your listening lesson today involves focus and concentration. Start near, go far, then lock in on any one sound that interests you. Keep listening to that sound. Listen exclusively to that sound, lock in on it and hear it in every rich dimension. Active listening is an exercise. Your ability to pay attention to individual sounds is teaching you a critical communication skill.

Thought for the Day:
Active listeners are the most welcomed participants in any conversation.

CHAPTER NINETEEN

Be Careful, the Truth Hurts

Little Johnny's mother was trying to explain the difference between the truth and a lie. Johnny was confused because his mother told him never to lie, but when a salesman came knocking at the door she told him to say that she wasn't home. His mother explained that sometimes what seems like a lie isn't a lie. She said that although she was in the house, when Johnny told the salesman that she wasn't home, it wasn't a lie because she wasn't home for the salesman. Johnny said he thought he understood, but it wasn't until years later that he truly comprehended what his mother was trying to teach him. Johnny's moral dilemma helps demonstrate the fine line between being literal and using common sense.

We all know people who pride themselves on their ability to "tell it like it is." They often blurt out the first thing that comes to mind, regardless of the consequences. If you are one of those people, you may be proud that you "don't pull any punches," but it's also likely that you sometimes leave a path of devastation in your wake. While it is generally a good idea to tell the truth, the whole truth, and nothing but the truth, there are times when self-editing before speaking is an appropriate course of action.

In 1993, David Koresh, and the Branch Davidians were involved in a shootout with ATF agents attempting to serve a warrant at their compound in Waco, Texas. Koresh and his group opened fire, killing four agents and wounding sixteen others.

The ATF had evidence that Koresh was stockpiling weapons, sleeping with underage girls, and leading an unorthodox life. He had multiple wives and impregnated women and girls while insisting that the other male members of his group remain celibate. Koresh believed that he was the Lamb of God destined to interpret the Seven Seals from the Book of Revelation. He was, in his own mind, a Messiah come to save the world.

The night of the shootout, Sunday, February 28, the Davidians called the radio station I managed. Earlier in the day, the ATF asked us to broadcast a message so Koresh would know that they were accepting a cease fire. We did what they asked, and the ATF went in to collect their dead and wounded. When the call came from the Davidians that night, I first spoke with Koresh's right hand man Steve Schneider. I tried to convince him to come out and bring along the women and children who were holed up in the compound. Steve was reluctant to answer my questions, so he handed the phone to Koresh. We talked for about an hour. He did most of the talking. Koresh was (as my mother used to say) "nuttier than a fruitcake". He talked about himself in the past tense and referred to himself as the Lamb of God. He explained that he would be consumed by flames and that the birds of the air would feed upon his corpse. He spoke in a sort of biblical gibberish, so that to some it might sound as if he was speaking from the Bible. I tried to get him to answer questions, but he simply rambled on about the end times. At first, I called him David, but he didn't respond to his own name. In order to get his attention, I called him Lamb.

When he heard me calling him Lamb, he stopped, and for a few minutes he listened and responded to my questions. But that was short-lived, and before long he went back to rambling about the Seven Seals. When calling him Lamb stopped working, I switched to Lord. He responded to questions when I addressed him as Lord. At the end of our private "conversation" off the air, and after I came to the conclusion that there was little hope of me talking him back down to earth, I called the ATF agent-in-charge and told him that I was going to put Koresh on the air for a few minutes.

Two days later, I was asked to appear on the NBC *Today* show with Bryant Gumbel. The Branch Davidian standoff was the lead news story in this country and around the world. Some reported that Koresh was a law abiding citizen whose home had been attacked by U.S. government forces. Others reported that he was a child-molesting lunatic that was stockpiling weapons and ammunition as he prepared for a battle with the government. In his time on the phone with me, he made it clear that he intended to leave the world in a blaze of glory.

Over the years I've interviewed lots of people from CEOs, politicians and radical extremists to famous athletes, authors, and movie stars. Along the way I've interviewed many individuals who were, again to use my mother's words, "at least a half bubble off plumb." I learned early on not to pay attention to hearsay or reputation. Some interview subjects that I was excited to meet turned out to be jerks, and some people I was prepared not to like turned out to be wonderful people. It's always best to keep an open mind. When I talked with Koresh, I tried to give him the benefit of the doubt.

That didn't last long. He lost me by insisting that he was the Lamb of God. As I had done in previous interviews with mentally unstable people (Cosmic Lady in San Francisco comes to mind) I found it easier to just go with the flow and let him pretend to be whoever he wanted to be. There was no point in arguing with him, so I focused completely on trying to get him to release the children being held within the compound. I expressed to him that he had an interesting story and that if he surrendered he could share it with the world. He did release nineteen children that night, after we repeatedly read a biblical sounding statement he wrote about the Seven Seals, but it was obvious to me early on in our phone call that he had no intention of releasing any of his children or the other adults under his command.

I was convinced that he was armed, dangerous, and way off his rocker. But there was a hitch, and it speaks to Johnny's moral dilemma. At the time Bryant Gumbel was asking me questions, the Branch Davidians had access to the airwaves. They were monitoring TV and radio for stories about themselves. There was a reasonable chance that Koresh could be watching my interview. Since he was holding dozens of hostages including infants and children, the last thing I wanted to do was to say something that would set him off. I knew I had to tread lightly. So instead of reporting that Koresh was a raving maniac who had no intention of coming out of his compound alive, I dodged questions with unresponsive answers. "He has a message that he wants to deliver," I said. "He has strong convictions." Instead of sharing my fear that he was going to kill everyone around him so he could achieve martyrdom, I said he seemed committed to his cause and intent on getting a religious message to the world. Rather than risk becoming the spark that set him off by inserting myself and my observations into the story, I fudged my answers in a way that wasn't completely truthful.

If I could have known for certain that he wasn't watching that live telecast, I might have told viewers what I'm sharing here. But there were bigger issues at stake. My "truth" had the potential to threaten lives. My honesty might have set off a chain of events that would have resulted in more death. In the end, Koresh and his followers poured kerosene up and down the hallways of the Mt. Carmel compound and sent themselves to a fiery death. Conspiracy theorists would have you believe that the government had a sinister plot to kill innocent men, women, and children, but don't believe it.

Stockpiling weapons, impregnating twelve-year-old girls, and proclaiming yourself the Messiah aren't consistent with rational behavior. Koresh's rhetoric convinced me that he was going to die so the world would know and remember his name. He was the only one who could unlock the Seven Seals. Like Johnny, in the interest of the greater good, I stretched the truth.

You may never have to make that kind of life or death decision on live television, but you will find yourself in a position to blow things up with the truth. If your friend has food on her mouth during a meal, it's a good idea to tell her. If she put on 20 pounds since you last saw her, it's probably better to compliment her outfit and avoid rubbing her nose in her weight problem. Sometimes the truths that we observe are better left unsaid.

Exercise 19

Listen today for at least ten minutes to what
you hear. Focus on sounds and invite them in.
What are they? Where are they coming from?
What do they mean? Connect with them.
If you were there, with the sounds you are
hearing, would they change? Try to listen and
observe without interfering.

Thought for the Day:
*The truth can be dangerous and painful. Some truths
are better left unsaid.*

CHAPTER TWENTY

A Quiet Little Voice

Agnes was a small child with big plans. When she was eight, her father's death set her on a journey. At twelve her inner voice directed her to become a missionary and travel to the Far East. When she was eighteen she left Macedonia, traveled to Ireland, and learned to speak English. A year later she moved to Calcutta, learned Bengali, and began teaching at a convent school. She became a nun and changed her name to Teresa. She taught for twenty years and rose to the position of head mistress. Sister Teresa wasn't satisfied. A quiet voice from within pushed her on. One day while she was praying, the voice told her to serve the poor. At that moment, Agnes became Mother Teresa. She recruited thousands of women who patterned their lives after hers, and today they minister to the poor in over a hundred countries around the world touching millions of lives.

I met Mother Teresa in San Francisco. I wanted to meet her, so I talked my boss into broadcasting her speech from St. Mary's Cathedral on the radio. As a co-anchor of the broadcast I got to sit close. She was old and wrinkled and a bit stooped over, but there was a sparkle in her eyes. The microphone was set for a person of normal height, too high for a woman less than five feet tall. We were concerned that the audio might not be clear. When she began to speak, magic settled over the crowd. Although she spoke in barely a whisper, everyone listening on the radio and everyone in the huge church heard her words loud and clear. There was no feedback. Her voice was amplified. It was powerful. It seemed to come from a place deep within each of us. We felt her message. My co-anchor Stan Bunger, remarked that something very strange was happening. Her gentle whisper was more powerful than any loud voice I have ever heard.

When I was in eighth grade, six high school boys were riding around my hometown one night having a good time. Five were seniors and one was a junior. They were good kids known to be a little wild now and then. One of the boys, named Larry, asked the driver to stop the car. Larry got out and said "I'm going home."

"Come on," they encouraged him. "It's early, and we're going to have some fun."

But Larry said no and headed home. It was unusual because Larry was normally the life of the party. He was often the last man standing after a night on the town, but that night he simply excused himself and abruptly exited the car.

Asked later about his decision, Larry said he didn't know why he got out of the car. He has never been able to explain why he decided to get out. He had a feeling that he should go home, so he got out and walked home.

On a county highway just north of town, the car he left reached speeds estimated at one hundred miles an hour. The wreckage from the collision was gruesome. The boys collided with a pickup truck. The old man driving the truck and the five boys in the car died instantly in a ball of fire. I remember seeing the mangled remains of the burned-out car after the accident. It smelled like death.

I heard my little voice fairly frequently when I was a child. It didn't direct me to be a missionary or found a religious order, and I don't remember it ever telling me to get out of a car. But when I paid attention, it served me quite well. Those little voices work best when we are quiet and reflective. Given the opportunity, little voices inside us can inspire us. Sometimes they whisper great ideas. When we listen carefully they help us make good decisions. If you've lost touch with your inner voice, you may need to find a quiet place to try to find it. *Your quiet voice lives in your peaceful reflection zone.* Sometimes it's in your dreams, sometimes it comes when you're completely awake. I've had people who have heard it while driving in their car. You can recognize it because it's always clear, and it comes as a small whisper. Your character, your brand, your reputation and your legacy are all connected to that whisper.

Sometimes avoiding stupid mistakes is as simple as listening to that quiet little voice. I've never heard anyone lecture about it, and I've never read about it in a book, but everyone I've asked has admitted to hearing it at one time or another. Ignore your quiet little voice at your own peril. People have walked away at the gate only to learn that their scheduled flight crashed without them. People inadvertently take detours only to find missing information or long lost friends. People imagine conversations with loved ones moments before the phone rings. There are myriad stories about crew members who stayed in port prior to a shipwreck, or workers who changed shifts at factories prior to explosions. These seemingly random occurrences happen with some regularity even though there is no common thread between those that are saved. All we know for certain is that sometimes we hear the little voice and heed the warning, and sometimes we ignore it and press ahead.

Isn't it amazing that we are equipped with a silent alarm system that alerts us to certain dangerous situations? Do you remember the last time you heard the voice tell you turn here or stay home or skip an appointment?

I've never heard of a situation where someone listened to their little voice and later felt regret, but there are numerous experiences in my own life where I've ignored the voice and wished that I had listened. Sometimes the voice tells us to take a chance, sometimes it encourages us to be cautious. Larry wasn't exactly sure what the voice said, but he knew he had to get out of the car, and that decision saved his life. Agnes didn't know that she would become Mother Teresa and impact millions of people, she just followed her inner voice one step at a time.

How do I know when to listen to the voice and trust my gut feeling? How do I know when to analyze every angle or make a snap decision? For me, some of the best decisions I've ever made came without extensive analysis. I've made some very good decisions in the moment because it just felt right. On the other hand, I've made some enormously bad decisions that I agonized over for days and weeks. The biggest and most important decisions in life are often the ones we agonize over. *If we "analyze" long enough we can talk ourselves into or out of almost anything.* So how is a person to decide?

Life experience shows us what is right and what is wrong. Your instincts are almost always right. Consider the factors involved in the decision, but don't overanalyze. Don't go against your gut instincts. Don't get caught up in internally debating moral decisions. You know what's right. Trying to justify the wrong decision leads to the most damaging mistakes. Trusting your gut and listening to the quiet whisper is always better than spending an inordinate amount of time in mental gymnastics.

But wait a minute! Didn't I say earlier that we should slow down? Didn't I suggest concentrating on decisions like we concentrate on breathing? Isn't there a contradiction in "trusting your gut" and "using your brain"?

In my life, especially when I consider the big decisions that changed things for the better or for the worse, the pattern is clear. For example, when I meet someone, I instinctively know if they are trustworthy. I've changed my mind about liking or not liking someone, but rarely is my gut wrong about values like trust and honesty. Most of the time, I can tell within 15 seconds if I trust a person or not. And it's not just physical. I've met people over the phone or through emails that I've "sensed" are good people, and invariably my gut instinct proves to be correct.

Scam artists may use the same words and some of the same techniques as honest people, but there's always a clue to their intentions. Pay close attention to everything and everyone, and even if you've been gullible in the past, you'll learn to distinguish. Just because a person puts on a happy face doesn't change his intentions or what's in her heart. Don't let your intellect or your emotions overpower your instincts.

I'm sure my gut has been wrong on occasion, and I've mistaken my own voice for the quiet little voice. There are people I've trusted who turned out to be untrustworthy. I've made my share of bad decisions about people and situations. But more often than not, it's been because I intentionally or subconsciously overlooked obvious signs. It's easy to be influenced by charismatic people who talk about the wonderful things they can do. It's easy to be impressed by a resume, reputation or endorsement. But when it comes to making big decisions, our own first reaction is generally associated with the best decision.

Sometimes that involves taking chances. You probably know people who have made bold decisions outside their comfort zones and reaped great rewards. I once quit my job and moved to an island for a year with no job and no income. It was a gut decision. The little voice said go for it, and I did. In retrospect it was one of the best moves I ever made. I've taken jobs and moved halfway across the country to places I'd never seen several times without regret. I went to live at a monastery for seven months. Some family and friends thought I was crazy, but living the peaceful life of a monk changed me in ways I could never have imagined. Many great inventors, creators and captains of industry proceeded in unusual directions, driven by their instincts, their gut, or that quiet little voice that only they could hear. Mother Teresa left home, traveled thousands of miles and touched millions of people. She also spent time every day in quiet reflection.

Each of us has a natural rhythm. Some are faster and quicker, some are slower and more deliberate. Find your rhythm and trust your instincts. When you regularly take time to decompress, to be thoughtful and meditative, it's a lot easier to make decisions under pressure. If your world is full of noise, commotion and stress, it's considerably more difficult to hear the voice or get in touch with your instincts. Bad decisions boil up out of allowing our brain to talk us into doing things that we instinctively know are wrong. If it's too good to be true, it's not true.

Don't be afraid. It's your life and you are ultimately responsible for it. *You know right from wrong, and you must learn to trust your instincts.*

Exercise 20

Take a moment and reflect about your best friends, the ones you trust. Can you remember your feelings when you first met? Now think about someone who disappointed you or betrayed you. Remember your first meeting. Was there a feeling at that first meeting that should have alerted you about what was to come?

Your listening exercise should be automatic by now. Sit quietly. Close your eyes. Hear the sounds that are around you. Push into the distance and listen for sounds that are further away. Listen for the most distant sound. Hear it as clearly as you can. Sounds are like life, they begin with and around you, and they extend as far as your imagination.

Thought for the Day:
It's hard to pay attention to your "quiet little voice" when you are distracted by noise. Be still.

CHAPTER TWENTY ONE

Time's a Wastin'

Mike was my best friend. He was strong as an ox before he was diagnosed with bladder cancer. Doctors operated and treated Mike with chemotherapy and radiation, but Mike died a horrible death. It was hard to watch him attempt to deal with unthinkable pain and suffering. His body was decimated, and he was reduced to nearly a skeleton. The worst part of Mike's death was watching him grow more and more afraid of dying. Mike was fearless in life, but when he faced death, the fear destroyed him. In his last days, we cried together. His body was full of cancer, and his heart was full of regret. He couldn't come to grips with his mistakes. He feared for his family. He had no anchor to hold him as he drifted closer and closer to the edge of death. In a final desperate gasp, he asked, "How do I pray?"

Mike never had religion. He never went to church and he never prayed. He believed there was a God, but he didn't know much about Him. He never tried to communicate with God. Then, in the shadow of death, he desperately asked me to teach him to pray. I prayed with Mike, but the pain of cancer was too strong. He couldn't find anything in my words to bring him comfort. It was too late for Mike to learn new thoughts.

In many ways, Mike is the inspiration for this book. His desperate desire to clean the slate ended in pain and disappointment. Peace was beyond his grasp.

We are all going to die. It will be a shame—and a catastrophically stupid mistake—if we don't prepare. Not having a plan for facing death is the one stupid mistake you really don't want to make.

When you're standing on the last rung, teetering on the brink of life and death, it's a little late to start thinking about stupid mistakes. Death is a great equalizer. It spares no one. Waiting till your time comes before finding peace with who you are is fraught with danger. What if you can't choose the time and day? What if death comes sneaking in like a thief in the night? Is your house in order? Do your loved ones know how you feel about them? Have you squared things with those who you have wronged? Have you asked for forgiveness? Are you ready to die?

A friend once asked me to visit her grandmother in the hospital. When I arrived the nurse on duty asked if I was family. I explained that I was only a friend of the family. She said, "Marie is dying. Do you mind sitting with her?" It was one of those decisions that I'll never forget. I held Marie's hand for about a half hour. It was obvious that death was near, and I felt a calm come over me. I comforted her and assured her that she was going to be just fine. I told her that she was going to a better place where there was no pain or suffering. She smiled. As she was looking into my eyes, she looked through me, above and beyond me, and passed on.

While I can't prove there's life after death any more than you can prove there isn't, I believe that I felt her spirit move beyond space and time. Marie's last gaze was somewhere beyond this world. It wasn't a blank stare, she was looking at something that drew her attention. My sister sat with my mom and reported the same feeling when my mother passed. People who prepare for the next life tend to exit this life peacefully. Those who don't prepare are left to fight and claw their way into the great unknown.

As Grannie Clampett in the 1960's TV show *The Beverly Hillbillies* used to say, "time's a wastin'." That was her way of telling her family to hurry up and get a move on, and it's appropriate in our final lesson. The reason we seek to eliminate stupid mistakes is to avoid the most serious stupid mistake you could make—failing to prepare for the certainty of death.

When the tornado siren sounds, you head for the basement. When the hurricane evacuation notice is issued, you move to higher ground. When the railroad crossing lights start flashing, it's time to clear the tracks. Don't wait till the eleventh hour. When you are prepared for the certainty of death, every day you live is a blessing.

People who have near-death experiences often report seeing a bright light at the end of a tunnel. Most times they come out of the experience with a new appreciation for everything and everyone. They change their behavior to reflect a new perspective. Don't wait to see the light. Spend a few minutes thinking about your mistakes, and a few more minutes thinking about the ramifications of what you've done. Learn from those mistakes and solidify a better life plan. Be still. Listen for that quiet little voice.

A monk named Benjamin once suggested that the best prayer is "I surrender." Surrender is another way to express how it feels to go beyond pretending. Surrender means hearing and appreciating the internal mechanism that guides us. Surrender is getting beyond wants and complaints, fears and disappointments. Surrender means acknowledging that we are all flawed, and we all make stupid mistakes. Surrender means letting it all go as you awake with a consciousness of your decisions and their outcomes. Surrender to the little voice that tells you what to do and what not to do. Chart a new course today. Climb the ladder toward a better life, filled with good decisions and fewer stupid mistakes.

King Solomon inherited a vast kingdom with many opportunities and a significant number of challenges. One night while Solomon was sleeping, he had a dream. In his dream, God promised him one wish. Solomon could have wished for a long life, wealth, or power. He could have asked for anything, but he wished only for an understanding heart that would allow him to distinguish right from wrong. Solomon became the wisest ruler the world has ever known. We still refer to "the wisdom of Solomon."

Surrender to the truth. The wants and needs, cares and thoughts of others are every bit as important as yours. Wish for good things for others as often as you wish things for yourself. Einstein used imagination to unlock universal secrets. Solomon wished for an understanding heart to know right from wrong. Wish for good decisions. Imagine doing the right thing.

Take notice of the little miracles around you every day. When your friend calls you at precisely the instant you were thinking of her, or when you both say the same word at the same instant, take note. When you instinctively take a different route and end up avoiding traffic or when you are short of money and an insurance check shows up in your mailbox, say "thank you" out loud. When those dozens of other wonderful things happen, just in time, that you can't explain, recognize and acknowledge them and be thankful. Being aware of and getting in touch with your inner voice enables you to connect with the life force that's been inside you from the beginning of time.

Preventing stupid mistakes is as easy as listening to your inner voice. It's as easy as recognizing that you are not the center of the universe. You are not the beginning and the end but a single point on the eternal timeline, connected to all things that came before and are still to come. You are uniquely responsible for you. Your thoughts, words and actions belong to you. Make certain they benefit others. Feel the unbridled joy of helping others. Meet someone for the first time and feel as if you've known them all your life. Hear new music and know that you've always loved it. Wish to see a falling star, a flower bloom, or to see a dolphin break the surface of the water and then take time, wait and watch it happen. Feel the presence of a close friend even when no one is near. Stop concentrating on their flaws and begin to see people as if they were what they could be. Choose wisely. Be conscious of each decision and feel wisdom growing in your heart.

Exercise 20

Every day requires a period of silent reflection and listening. Make it part of your routine, as important as breakfast or drinking water. Your mind needs listening time to block out the noise of the world and help you concentrate. Listen to every sound you can hear. Listen especially for your quiet little voice.

Thought for the Day:
The decisions we pray about, the ones that rely on our "quiet little voice" create harmony, happiness and peace. Be still and be good.

Charlie Seraphin Biography

Over the past forty years, Charlie Seraphin has been a journalist, a radio host, a sports executive, and a college professor. He has interviewed hundreds of notable people, including Ronald Reagan, Yogi Berra, Dr. Benjamin Spock, Barbara Bush and David Koresh. A native of rural Wisconsin, he has lived all over the world—from San Francisco and London to Ibiza and Texas. He and his wife Dianne have six adult children and four grandchildren.

Acknowledgements

Special thanks to two incredible friends, JW Babcock whose support and encouragement brought this project to print, and John Granville Leonard who believed from the beginning, pushing and gently directing my efforts. To Anne Trubek for bringing my dream to life. To Dan Crissman who morphed a manuscript into a finished product. To Dianne who provided me time to write, and Noelle who critiqued my earliest attempts. To Dave and Stan and Tharon and Don and Kathy and friends from coast to coast who encouraged me. Special thanks to my late friend Mike Marak, and all departed friends and relatives watching from above. May you rest in peace. Those who passed before provided the impetus for this book. And much love to all of you who read. Your decision has already made our world a better place.

CPSIA information can be obtained
at www.ICGtesting.com
Printed in the USA
LVHW092016051118
595973LV00009B/438/P